Pomchi Pr

Pomchi Book

of

Cars, Vans

&

Light Trucks

Volume 2

Japan 1935 to 1939

Edited by Jeremy Risdon

Contents

Introduction 5
Coverage 5
Key to data panels 6
Abbreviations 8
Asahi (Miyata Works) 9
Asia 9
Atsuta (Chukyo Detroit Project) 11
Chrysler (Chrysler Automobile Works) 11
Crabbe 11
Daihatsu (Hatsudoki Seizo) 13
Denka (Nippon Electric Car) 17
Ford (Ford Japan) 17
Fujiya 26
General Motors Japan: Chevrolet 26
General Motors Japan: Pontiac/Oldsmobile 29
Giant (Seiki Kogyo) 31
Harley Davidson 33
Hijiri 33
Hirano (Hirano Seizakusho) 33
Hitachi-Federal 35
Hitakashi 35
Hoxon 35
Hyogo (HMC) 37
Ikegai (Kawasaki Machinery Co) 37
Isuzu (Tokyo Automobile Industries Co) 39
Isuzu: Chiyoda (Tokyo Gas and Electric) 44
Isuzu: Sumida (Jidosha Kogyo) 44
Iwasaki (Asahi Nainenki) 50

JAC	52
Kokueki	52
Kurakawa	52
Kurogane: New Era (Nihon Jidosha)	54
Kurogane (Nihon Nainenki)	54
Kyoho	60
Kyosan (Kyosan Electric Manufacturing Co)	61
Matsuo	65
Mazda (Matsuda)	65
Mitsubishi (Mitsubishi Heavy Industries)	70
Miyata (Miyata Works)	70
Mizuno Metal Works	70
MSA	72
Nagoya (Nagoya Automotive Works)	72
Nakajima (Nakajima Seisakusho/Yuasa Battery)	72
Nichiden (NEC Automotive Works)	75
Nikko	75
Nissan: Datsun (Nissan Motor Co)	77
Nissan (Nissan Motor Co)	94
Nissin/Nisso	107
Noritu	107
Ohta (Kohsoku Kikan Kogyo)	109
Okamoto	115
OS	115
Raito (Raito Automobile Co)	115
Rikuo (Rikuo Nainenki)	118
Rokko (Kawasaki Rolling Stock)	118
Showa-Go	122
Success (Osawa Shokai)	122
Suzuki	122

Takara	122
Toyota: Toyoda Automatic Loom Works (cars)	124
Toyota (Toyota Motor Co) (cars)	129
Toyota: Toyoda Automatic Loom Works (commercials)	129
Toyota (Toyota Motor Co) (commercials)	137
Tsubasa (NABCO)	140
Tsukuba (Tokyo Jidosha Seizo)	142
Welby (KRS)	142
Yamarta (Osaka Minata Nakijima Seisakusho)	142
Bibliography	145
Image sources	146

Also available:

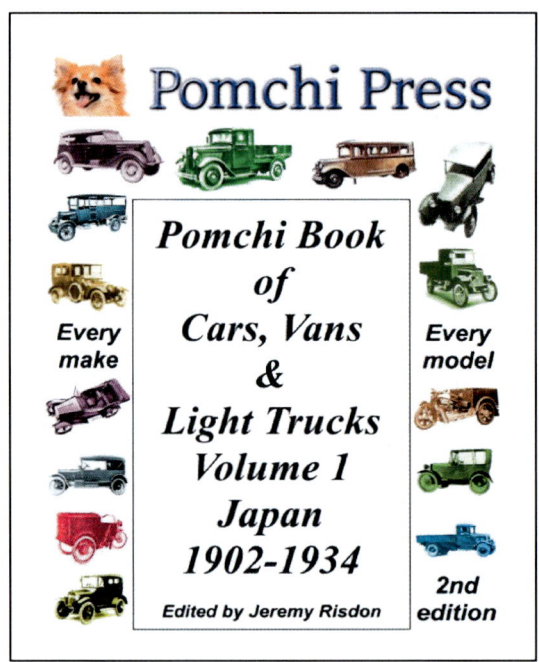

Introduction

This is the second volume in the Pomchi Press series that aims to provide a basic catalogue of every make and model of car and light commercial vehicle produced. This is of course an impossible task and while I would not claim that this volume is 100% complete or accurate it should serve as a useful resource on the subject matter.

This volume, covering model series introduced in Japan between 1935 and 1939, reflects the decline of the American marques over this period and the increasing strength of the domestic Japanese brands. Military vehicles remain significant and this volume also covers numerous small manufacturers of three wheel sanrinsha (motor tricycles) and small electric vehicles.

Representative images have been included (where available), poor quality images have been included in preference to nothing at all. Images for assembled vehicles have only been included where a Japanese market version has been identified or featured in Japanese market literature even if the vehicle is not specific to the Japanese market.

Research for this volume has highlighted that a lot of the information uncovered on the subject matter is conflicting and this volume has been prepared on the basis of the information presented being the best interpretation of what was available at the time of publication.

Jeremy Risdon, Editor.

Coverage

Grey areas relevant to this volume:

Vehicle type	Coverage
Light commercials	Light commercial definitions vary. A 1t payload/3.5t gvw is usually considered a light commercial and a 3t payload/7.5t gvw not. This volume aims for a flexible limit of around 2t payload/5.5t gvw for inclusion.
Military vehicles	Included up to light commercial definition limit but excluding specialist applications.
Prototypes	Significant models included where identified.
Three wheelers	Included if designed as a three wheeler with specific bodywork or frame for this purpose including those with a motorbike base. Motorbikes with an added wheel arrangement are not included; likewise pedal three wheeler vehicles with an accessory motor attachment.
Two wheelers	Excluded.
Specialist application vehicles	Excluded. E.g. vehicles intended for construction, farming and municipal use.
Minibuses	Included if a product of the chassis manufacturer up to 15 seats - higher if a variation of an existing light commercial listing. Specialist bodywork companies have not been included.

Key to data panels

Individual entries may not contain all sections of these panels.

Layout 1

Model group				1				
Model sub group				2				
Marque				Model				
3				4				
Body type(s)		5		5		5		
Power units	6	6		6	6	Timeline		
Final assembly:		Key market	Length (cm)		Drive	Intro.	Start	End	LOST
7	8	9	10		11	12	13	14	15
Variations: 16								

Layout 2 - American manufacturers multiple assembled models list

Model group				1				
Final assembly:		7			8			
Marque			3		Timeline			
Model	MY	Body type		Power unit	Intro.	Start	End	LOST
4	17	5		6	12	13	14	15

1. Model group – e.g. Toyota GA; Toyota GY; Toyota DA

High level model group as designated in originating country. Each significant model revision has a different model group and models are listed as original, or revised with the modification year. Marque changes are treated as continuations.

2. Model Sub group – e.g. Toyota GA

The model sub group is used for a group within the main group.

3. Marque – e.g. Toyota

Marque name variation was marketed under.

4. Model – e.g. GA

Model designation variation was marketed under.

5. Body type(s) – e.g. Truck

Body style(s) of the variation.

6. Power units – e.g. 3389(65)

Power unit options for the variation. These will be normally aspirated petrol unless there is a sub designation (e.g. D for Diesel). Power output figures are in brackets (where available).

7. Final assembly

Country of final assembly.

8. Plant

Location of final assembly plant.

9. Key market – e.g. Export

Primary market for the variation. This will be Japan for vehicles aimed at the Japanese market including those that were also exported. Export is used for variations sold only outside of Japan.

10. Length

Length in centimetres.

11. Drive

Drive layout of variation (see abbreviations list).

12. Intro

Public launch year – start of timeline for the model.

13. Start

Production start year.

14. End

Production finish year.

15. LOST

Last On Sale Traced – end of variation timeline.

16. Variations – e.g. std, Special, De Luxe

Where available, specific model variations have been listed.

17. Model year

Model year for American assembled models. This may differ from timeline dates.

Abbreviations

4wd – 4 wheel drive

BMR – Bike type, Mid engine, Rear wheel drive

Cyl – Cylinder

Dr – Door

E (in power unit) - Electric

FF – front engine, front wheel drive

FR – front engine, rear wheel drive

F4 – front engine, four wheel drive

F6x4 – front engine, four wheel drive, six wheels

gvw – gross vehicle weight

hp – horse power

JDM – Japanese Domestic Market

JP – Japan

LOST – Last On Sale Traced

lwb – long wheelbase

MY – Model year

P (in power unit) - PS

P (in timeline) – Prototype, date entry does not apply

R (in timeline) – Racing model, date entry does not apply

Std – Standard

swb – short wheelbase

T – ton

V – V formation engine

w/b – wheelbase

Asahi (Miyata Works)

The Asahi was a small car in the roadster/scout car style. Produced by Miyata, a cycle maker that also made trucks under the Miyata name. The Asahi Roadster had an air cooled V-twin engine and all round independent suspension.

Model group	Asahi							
Marque	Model							
Asahi	16hp							
Body type(s)	Roadster							
Power units	730(16)				Timeline			
Final assembly:	Key market	Length (cm)	Drive	Intro.	Start	End	LOST	
Japan	Tokyo	Japan		FF	1937	1937	1939	1939

Asia

Contemporary three wheel cycle based truck manufacturer. Estimated production dates. Minor changes over the period covered.

Model group	Asia Go original							
Marque	Model							
Asia	Go							
Body type(s)	3 wheel cycle truck							
Power units	744(7.5)				Timeline			
Final assembly:	Key market	Length (cm)	Drive	Intro.	Start	End	LOST	
Japan	Japan			BMR	1937	1937	1938	1938

Model group	Asia Go revised 1938							
Marque	Model							
Asia	Go							
Body type(s)	3 wheel cycle truck							
Power units	744(7.5)				Timeline			
Final assembly:	Key market	Length (cm)	Drive	Intro.	Start	End	LOST	
Japan	Japan			BMR	1938	1938	1939	1939

Asahi

Asahi Roadster

Asia

Asia-Go

1937 above,
1938 right

Atsuta (Chukyo Detroit Project)

Atsuta was a joint effort between several companies: Nippon Sharyo Ltd. created the frame and body, Okamoto Bicycle Works provided the wheels and braking system, while Toyoda Loom Company was responsible for the cast parts. The Atsuta was an expensive car with 8 cylinder engines and USA lookalike styling. Production was around 40 units with individual specifications in sedan and phaeton format made between 1932 and 1937.

Model group			Atsuta					
Marque			Model					
Atsuta			Sedan					
Body type(s)	Sedan 4dr		Phaeton 4dr					
Power units	3933(85)					Timeline		
Final assembly:		Key market	Length (cm)		Drive	Intro.	Start	End	LOST
Japan	Nagoya	Japan			FR	1935	1935	1937	1937

Atsuta models available in this period covered in previous volumes:
- Atsuta Sedan revised 1934, 1934-1935, Volume 1
- Atsuta Phaeton (original), 1933-1935, Volume 1

Chrysler (Chrysler Automobile Works)

Chrysler assembled (in Shibaura, Tokyo) and also imported vehicles to Japan between 1927 and 1939. Products included models from Chrysler, De Soto, Dodge and Plymouth car ranges along with Dodge and Fargo trucks. Insufficient information has been found on assembled models available to provide more detailed coverage.

Also see the Ford section which covers the decline of the American assembly plants in Japan during the period covered by this volume.

Crabbe

Model group			Crabbe					
Marque			Model					
Crabbe			Rear-Car					
Body type(s)	3 wheel cycle truck							
Power units	500(5)					Timeline		
Final assembly:		Key market	Length (cm)		Drive	Intro.	Start	End	LOST
Japan		Japan			BMR	Circa 1935			

Atsuta

Atsuta Phaeton

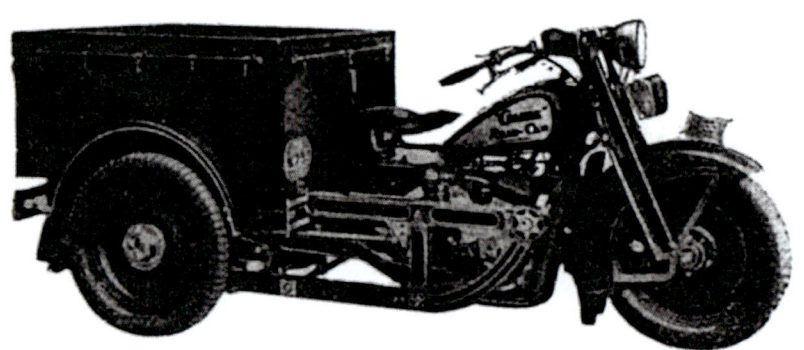

Atsuta Sedans 1935 (above), unknown year left

Crabbe

Rear-Car

Daihatsu (Hatsudoki Seizo)

Daihatsu continued to evolve their sanrinsha series and started to experiment with four wheel models in scout car and truck formats. Model differences are outlined on the picture pages.

Model group		Daihatsu 3 wheeler H series revised 1935						
Model sub group		Daihatsu HS						
Marque		Model						
Daihatsu		HS						
Body type(s)	3 wheel cycle truck							
Power units	498	670	744		Timeline			
Final assembly:		Key market	Length (cm)	Drive	Intro.	Start	End	LOST
Japan	Osaka	Japan	278	BMR	1935	1935	1937	1937

Model group		Daihatsu 3 wheeler H series revised 1935						
Model sub group		Daihatsu HS						
Marque		Model						
Daihatsu		HS Rickshaw						
Body type(s)	3 wheel rickshaw							
Power units	498	670	744		Timeline			
Final assembly:		Key market	Length (cm)	Drive	Intro.	Start	End	LOST
Japan	Osaka	Japan		BMR	1936	1936	1937	1937

Model group		Daihatsu 3 wheeler H series revised 1935						
Model sub group		Daihatsu HQ						
Marque		Model						
Daihatsu		HQ						
Body type(s)	3 wheel cycle truck							
Power units	744				Timeline			
Final assembly:		Key market	Length (cm)	Drive	Intro.	Start	End	LOST
Japan	Osaka	Japan		BMR	1935	1935	1937	1937

Model group		Daihatsu 3 wheeler S-series original						
Model sub group		Daihatsu SA						
Marque		Model						
Daihatsu		SA						
Body type(s)	3 wheel cycle truck							
Power units	498	670	736		Timeline			
Final assembly:		Key market	Length (cm)	Drive	Intro.	Start	End	LOST
Japan	Osaka	Japan	278	BMR	1937	1937	1938	1938

Daihatsu models available in this period covered in previous volumes:
- Daihatsu HT, 1934-1935, Volume 1

Daihatsu

HS

HS is improved version of earlier HT model recognised by sculpted disc wheels.

HQ is extended version using 736cc engine.

HS Rickshaw

SB

SA

SA and SB models feature revised design recognised by new frame graphic (forward sloping on SA, back sloping on SB). SB drops 498cc version. SSA and SSB are extended high capacity models with 736cc engine.

Daihatsu (Hatsudoki Seizo)

Model group	\multicolumn{6}{c}{Daihatsu 3 wheeler S-series original}
Model sub group	Daihatsu SA					
Marque	Model					
Daihatsu	SSA					
Body type(s)	3 wheel cycle truck					
Power units	736				Timeline	
Final assembly:		Key market	Length (cm)	Drive	Intro.	Start	End	LOST
Japan	Osaka	Japan		BMR	1937	1937	1938	1938

Model group	Daihatsu 3 wheeler S-series revised 1938
Model sub group	Daihatsu SB
Marque	Model
Daihatsu	SB
Body type(s)	3 wheel cycle truck
Power units	670 / 736

Final assembly:		Key market	Length (cm)	Drive	Intro.	Start	End	LOST
Japan	Osaka	Japan	278	BMR	1938	1938	1940	1940

Model group	Daihatsu 3 wheeler S-series revised 1938
Model sub group	Daihatsu SB
Marque	Model
Daihatsu	SSB
Body type(s)	3 wheel cycle truck
Power units	736

Final assembly:		Key market	Length (cm)	Drive	Intro.	Start	End	LOST
Japan	Osaka	Japan		BMR	1938	1938	1940	1940

Model group	Daihatsu FRA
Marque	Model
Daihatsu	FRA
Body type(s)	Roadster
Power units	1200

Final assembly:		Key market	Length (cm)	Drive	Intro.	Start	End	LOST
Japan	Osaka			F4	1937	P	P	P

Model group	Daihatsu FA
Marque	Model
Daihatsu	FA
Body type(s)	Pick up
Power units	732

Final assembly:		Key market	Length (cm)	Drive	Intro.	Start	End	LOST
Japan	Osaka	Japan		FR	1937	1937	1939	1939

Daihatsu

FRA

FRA is small roadster prototype with 1200cc V2 engine. All wheel drive but some front drive models may also have been built.

FA is limited run small truck (around 200 units) equipped with a flat twin engine.

Daihatsu did not progress with four wheeled models after these limited experiments until some time after WWII.

FA

Denka

Denka made other electric models around this time. Pre 1940 production has been unconfirmed so these will appear in volume 3 of this series but may have been produced in the period covered by this volume.

Denka (Nippon Electric Car)

Model group	Denka						
Marque	Model						
Denka	Standard Sedan						
Body type(s)	Sedan 2dr						
Power units	E(2.75)				Timeline		
Final assembly:		Key market	Length (cm)	Drive	Intro.	Start	End	LOST
Japan	Amagasaki	Japan	280		1938	1938	1940	1940

Ford (Ford Japan)

All models assembled from imported kits.

Model group	Ford Model C 10 revised 1935						
Marque	Model						
Ford	10						
Body type(s)	Sedan 2dr		Sedan 4dr		Roadster		
Power units	1172(30)				Timeline		
Final assembly:		Key market	Length (cm)	Drive	Intro.	Start	End	LOST
Japan	Yokohama	Japan	369	FR	1936	1936	1937	1937

Model group	Ford V8 MY1935						
Marque	Model						
Ford	Model 48 V8						
Body type(s)	Tudor Sedan 2dr		Fordor Sedan 4dr		Coupe		
	Convertible 2dr		Roadster 2dr		Phaeton 4dr		
	Convertible Sedan 4dr						
Power units	3622(85)				Timeline		
Final assembly:		Key market	Length (cm)	Drive	Intro.	Start	End	LOST
Japan	Yokohama	Japan	464	FR	1935	1935	1935	1935
Variations: std (Tudor, Fordor, Coupe); De Luxe							

Model group	Ford V8 MY1936						
Marque	Model						
Ford	Model 68 V8						
Body type(s)	Tudor Sedan 2dr		Tudor Trunk Sedan 2dr		Fordor Sedan 4dr		
	Fordor Trunk Sedan 4dr		Coupe 3 window		Coupe 5 window		
	Convertible 2dr		Roadster		Phaeton		
	Convertible Sedan 4dr						
Power units	3622(85)				Timeline		
Final assembly:		Key market	Length (cm)	Drive	Intro.	Start	End	LOST
Japan	Yokohama	Japan	464	FR	1935	1935	1936	1936
Variations: std (Tudor, Fordor, Coupe 5 window); De Luxe							

Ford

Revised version of British Ford Model C Ten.

Model Y also remained available until 1937.

10 Sedan 2dr

10 Sedan 4dr

Brochure cover

10 Roadster

Model 10

Ford (Ford Japan)

Model group		Ford V8 MY1937					
Marque		Model					
Ford		Model 71 V8					
Body type(s)		Tudor Sedan 2dr	Tudor Trunk Sedan 2dr		Fordor Sedan 4dr		
		Fordor Trunk Sedan 4dr	Coupe 5 window		Convertible 2dr		
		Roadster	Phaeton		Convertible Sedan 4dr		
Power units	3622(85)				Timeline		
Final assembly:		Key market	Length (cm)	Drive	Intro.	Start	End	LOST
Japan	Yokohama	Japan	456	FR	1936	1936	1937	1937
Variations: std (Tudor, Fordor, Coupe 5 window); De Luxe							

Model group		Ford V8 MY1938					
Marque		Model					
Ford		Model 81 V8					
Body type(s)		Tudor Sedan 2dr	Fordor Sedan 4dr		Coupe		
		Convertible 2dr	Roadster		Phaeton		
		Convertible Sedan 4dr					
Power units	3622(85)				Timeline		
Final assembly:		Key market	Length (cm)	Drive	Intro.	Start	End	LOST
Japan	Yokohama	Japan	456	FR	1937	1937	1938	1938
Variations: std (Tudor, Fordor, Coupe); De Luxe							

Model group		Ford V8 MY1939					
Marque		Model					
Ford		Model 91 V8					
Body type(s)		Tudor Sedan 2dr	Fordor Sedan 4dr		Coupe		
		Convertible 2dr					
Power units	3622(90)				Timeline		
Final assembly:		Key market	Length (cm)	Drive	Intro.	Start	End	LOST
Japan	Yokohama	Japan	456	FR	1938	1938	1940	1940
Variations: std (Tudor, Fordor, Coupe); De Luxe							

The American origin Ford models covered in this volume were similar to the US equivalents. Assembly was at the Koyasu plant in Yokohama as it had been from 1929 after taking over from the previous Midorimachi plant, also in Yokohama.

Ford

V8
Model 68
1936

2dr Trunk Sedan

2dr Sedan

4dr Sedan

4dr Trunk Sedan

Ford

V8
Model 68
1936

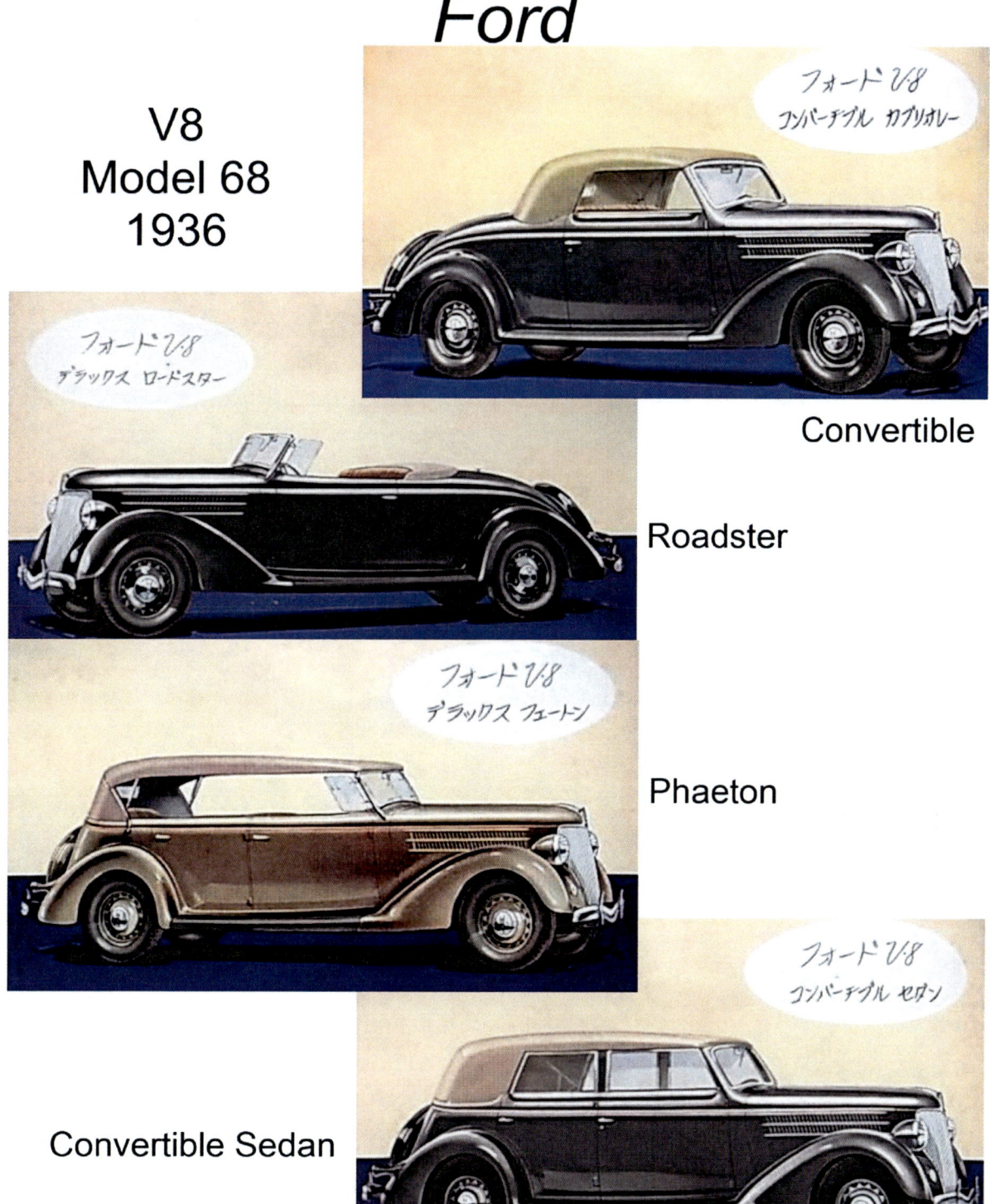

Convertible

Roadster

Phaeton

Convertible Sedan

Ford

V8
Model 68
1936

Coupe 3 Window

Coupe 5 Window

Commercials
1935

1935 sales brochure

Model 51 Truck

Ford (Ford Japan)

Model group	Ford V8 commercial (Express and Panel)						
Final assembly:	Japan			Yokohama			
Marque	Ford			Timeline			
Model	MY	Body type	Power unit	Intro.	Start	End	LOST
Model 50 V8 Standard	1935	Express pick up	3622(85)	1935	1935	1935	1935
Model 50 V8 Standard	1935	Panel van	3622(85)	1935	1935	1935	1935
Model 50 V8 De Luxe	1935	Panel van	3622(85)	1935	1935	1935	1935
Model 67 V8 Standard	1936	Express pick up	3622(85)	1935	1935	1936	1936
Model 67 V8 Standard	1936	Panel van	3622(85)	1935	1935	1936	1936
Model 67 V8 De Luxe	1936	Panel van	3622(85)	1935	1935	1936	1936
Model 77 V8 Standard	1937	Express pick up	3622(85)	1936	1936	1937	1937
Model 77 V8 Standard	1937	Panel van	3622(85)	1936	1936	1937	1937
Model 77 V8 De Luxe	1937	Panel van	3622(85)	1936	1936	1937	1937
Model 81C V8 Standard swb	1938	Express pick up	3622(85)	1937	1937	1938	1938
Model 81C V8 Standard swb	1938	Panel van	3622(85)	1937	1937	1938	1938
Model 81C V8 De Luxe swb	1938	Panel van	3622(85)	1937	1937	1938	1938
Model 81C V8 Standard lwb	1938	Express pick up	3622(85)	1937	1937	1938	1938
Model 81C V8 Standard lwb	1938	Panel van	3622(85)	1937	1937	1938	1938
Model 81C V8 De Luxe lwb	1938	Panel van	3622(85)	1937	1937	1938	1938
Model 91C V8 Standard swb	1939	Express pick up	3622(85)	1938	1938	1940	1940
Model 91C V8 Standard swb	1939	Panel van	3622(85)	1938	1938	1940	1940
Model 91C V8 De Luxe swb	1939	Panel van	3622(85)	1938	1938	1940	1940
Model 91C V8 Standard lwb	1939	Express pick up	3622(85)	1938	1938	1940	1940
Model 91C V8 Standard lwb	1939	Panel van	3622(85)	1938	1938	1940	1940
Model 91C V8 De Luxe lwb	1939	Panel van	3622(85)	1938	1938	1940	1940

This period 1935-1939 was a period of decline for the American brands. In 1936 the Ministry of Commerce and Industry, under pressure from the Army, enacted the Automobile Manufacturing Enterprise law which stipulated that producer licences should be applied to vehicle production. The Army wanted to remove reliance on the American companies so licences were only granted to the big Japanese producers (Nissan, Isuzu and Toyoda). The law also stipulated at least half the capital, company officials and shareholders should be Japanese and manufacturers should abide by the orders of the Army. In contrast to the licensed producer beneficial status, the American companies found themselves with restricted output and increased import duties. In 1939 following the passing of the Foreign Exchange Control Law production by US companies stopped altogether. American vehicles did not disappear entirely at this stage. Local management took over the assembly plants and many existing models remained available into the following decade. Dates in this volume are the best estimates of availability. Virtual copies of American models appeared under different brand names (JAC, Nikko) at the end of this period. These may have been produced in the former US plants but this is unconfirmed.

Ford (Ford Japan)

Model group		Ford V8 commercial (Truck and Chassis)					
Final assembly:		Japan			Yokohama		
Marque			Ford		Timeline		
Model	MY	Body type	Power unit	Intro.	Start	End	LOST
Model 51 V8 131½ inch	1935	Chassis	3622(85)	1935	1935	1936	1936
Model 51 V8 131½ inch	1935	Truck	3622(85)	1935	1935	1936	1936
Model 51 V8 131½ inch	1935	Stake Body Truck	3622(85)	1935	1935	1936	1936
Model 51 V8 157 inch (swb)	1935	Chassis	3622(85)	1935	1935	1936	1936
Model 51 V8 157 inch (swb)	1935	Truck	3622(85)	1935	1935	1936	1936
Model 51 V8 157 inch (swb)	1935	Stake Body Truck	3622(85)	1935	1935	1936	1936
Model 79 V8 134 inch (swb)	1937	Chassis	3622(85)	1936	1936	1937	1937
Model 79 V8 134 inch (swb)	1937	Truck	3622(85)	1936	1936	1937	1937
Model 79 V8 134 inch (swb)	1937	Stake Body Truck	3622(85)	1936	1936	1937	1937
Model 79 V8 157 inch (swb)	1937	Chassis	3622(85)	1936	1936	1937	1937
Model 79 V8 157 inch (swb)	1937	Truck	3622(85)	1936	1936	1937	1937
Model 79 V8 157 inch (swb)	1937	Stake Body Truck	3622(85)	1936	1936	1937	1937
Model 81T V8 134 inch (swb)	1938	Chassis	3622(85)	1937	1937	1938	1938
Model 81T V8 134 inch (swb)	1938	Truck	3622(85)	1937	1937	1938	1938
Model 81T V8 134 inch (swb)	1938	Stake Body Truck	3622(85)	1937	1937	1938	1938
Model 817T V8 157 inch	1938	Chassis	3622(85)	1937	1937	1938	1938
Model 817T V8 157 inch	1938	Truck	3622(85)	1937	1937	1938	1938
Model 817T V8 157 inch	1938	Stake Body Truck	3622(85)	1937	1937	1938	1938
Model 91T V8 134 inch (swb)	1939	Chassis	3622(85)	1938	1938	1940	1940
Model 91T V8 134 inch (swb)	1939	Truck	3622(85)	1938	1938	1940	1940
Model 91T V8 134 inch (swb)	1939	Stake Body Truck	3622(85)	1938	1938	1940	1940
Model 917T V8 157 inch	1939	Chassis	3622(85)	1938	1938	1940	1940
Model 917T V8 157 inch	1939	Truck	3622(85)	1938	1938	1940	1940
Model 917T V8 157 inch	1939	Stake Body Truck	3622(85)	1938	1938	1940	1940

Models available in this period covered in previous volumes:
Ford Model Y, 1932-1937, Volume 1
Ford 10 (original), 1934-1936, Volume 1
Ford Model B revised 1934, 1934-1935, Volume 1
Ford Model BB revised 1934, 1934-1935, Volume 1
Ford Model C, 1933-1935, Volume 1
Ford V8 Model 40, 1933-1935, Volume 1

Ford

Commercials
1938-1939

Model 81T Truck
1938

Model 81T
Chassis
1938

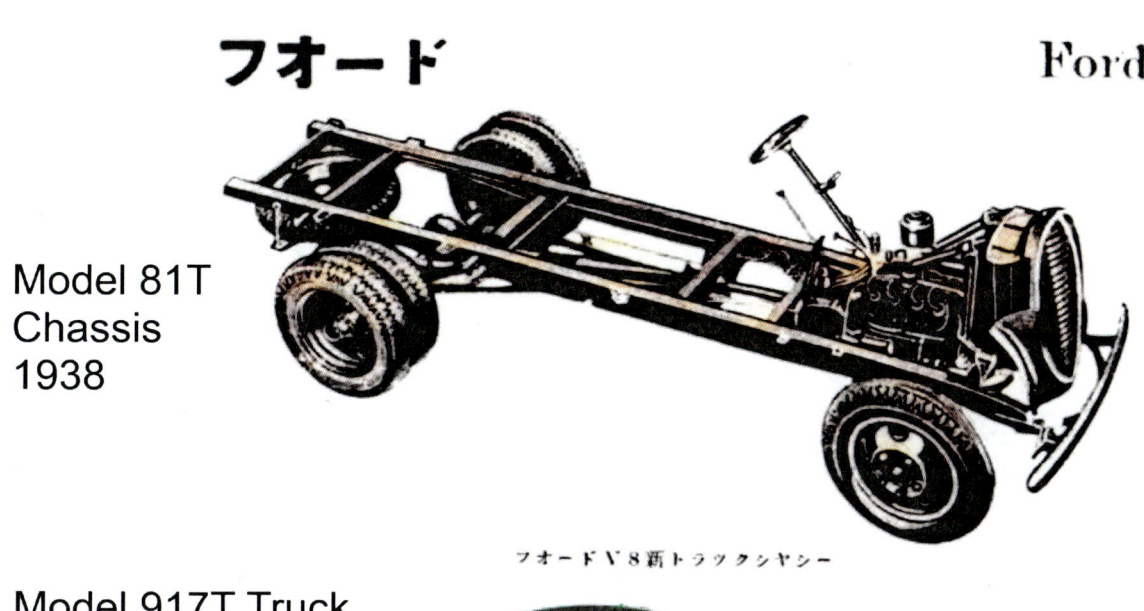

Model 917T Truck
1939

Fujiya

Model group	Fujiya 675cc original							
Marque	Model							
Fujiya	675cc							
Body type(s)	3 wheel cycle truck							
Power units	675				Timeline			
Final assembly:		Key market	Length (cm)	Drive	Intro.	Start	End	LOST
Japan	Tokyo	Japan	280	BMR	1937	1937	1939	1939
Variations: FA (side valve), FH (ohv)								

Model group	Fujiya 675cc revised 1939							
Marque	Model							
Fujiya	675cc							
Body type(s)	3 wheel cycle truck							
Power units	675				Timeline			
Final assembly:		Key market	Length (cm)	Drive	Intro.	Start	End	LOST
Japan	Tokyo	Japan	280	BMR	1939	1939	1939	1939
Variations: FA (side valve), FH (ohv)								

Models available in this period covered in previous volumes:
- Fujiya 650cc, 1934-1937, Volume 1

General Motors Japan: Chevrolet

All General Motors models were assembled from imported kits.

Model group	General Motors Japan							
Final assembly:	Japan				Osaka			
Marque			Chevrolet		Timeline			
Model	MY	Body type		Power unit	Intro.	Start	End	LOST
EC Series Standard Six	1935	Sedan 4dr		3389(74)	1935	1935	1935	1935
EC Series Standard Six	1935	Phaeton 4dr		3389(74)	1935	1935	1935	1935
ED Series Master	1935	Sedan 4dr		3389(80)	1935	1935	1935	1935
ED Series Master	1935	Sport Sedan 4dr		3389(80)	1935	1935	1935	1935
FD Series Master	1936	Sedan 4dr		3389(79)	1935	1935	1936	1936
FD Series Master	1936	Sport Sedan 4dr		3389(79)	1935	1935	1936	1936
GB Series Master	1937	Sedan 4dr		3548(85)	1936	1936	1937	1937
GB Series Master	1937	Sport Sedan 4dr		3548(85)	1936	1936	1937	1937
HB Series Master	1938	Sedan 4dr		3548(85)	1937	1937	1938	1938
HB Series Master	1938	Sport Sedan 4dr		3548(85)	1937	1937	1938	1938
JB Series Master	1939	Sedan 4dr		3548(85)	1938	1938	1940	1940
JB Series Master	1939	Sport Sedan 4dr		3548(85)	1938	1938	1940	1940

Fujiya

650cc 1936

675cc advert 1937

675cc 1937

675cc 1939

Later models came with disc wheels and option of side or overhead valves.

General Motors Japan: Chevrolet

Model group		General Motors Japan					
Final assembly:		Japan		Osaka			
Marque		Chevrolet		Timeline			
Model	MY	Body type	Power unit	Intro.	Start	End	LOST
EB Series 112 inch w/b	1935	Pick up	3389(80)	1935	1935	1935	1935
EB Series 112 inch w/b	1935	Chassis	3389(80)	1935	1935	1935	1935
QA Series 1½t 131 inch w/b	1935	Truck	3389(69)	1935	1935	1936	1936
QA Series 1½t 131 inch w/b	1935	Chassis	3389(69)	1935	1935	1936	1936
QB Series 1½t 131 inch w/b	1936	Truck	3389(69)	1935	1935	1936	1936
QB Series 1½t 131 inch w/b	1936	Chassis	3389(69)	1935	1935	1936	1936
QC Series 1½t 157 inch w/b	1935	Truck	3389(69)	1935	1935	1936	1936
QC Series 1½t 157 inch w/b	1935	Chassis	3389(69)	1935	1935	1936	1936
QD Series 1½t 157 inch w/b	1936	Truck	3389(69)	1935	1935	1936	1936
QD Series 1½t 157 inch w/b	1936	Chassis	3389(69)	1935	1935	1936	1936
FB Series 112 inch w/b	1936	Pick up	3389(80)	1935	1935	1936	1936
FB Series 112 inch w/b	1936	Chassis	3389(80)	1935	1935	1936	1936
GC Series 112 inch w/b	1937	Pick up	3548(85)	1936	1936	1937	1937
GC Series 112 inch w/b	1937	Chassis	3548(85)	1936	1936	1937	1937
RA Series 1½t 131 inch w/b	1937	Truck	3548(78)	1936	1936	1937	1937
RA Series 1½t 131 inch w/b	1937	Chassis	3548(78)	1936	1936	1937	1937
RB Series 1½t 131 inch w/b	1937	Truck	3548(78)	1936	1936	1937	1937
RB Series 1½t 131 inch w/b	1937	Chassis	3548(78)	1936	1936	1937	1937
RC Series 1½t 157 inch w/b	1937	Truck	3548(78)	1936	1936	1937	1937
RC Series 1½t 157 inch w/b	1937	Chassis	3548(78)	1936	1936	1937	1937
RD Series 1½t 157 inch w/b	1937	Truck	3548(78)	1936	1936	1937	1937
RD Series 1½t 157 inch w/b	1937	Chassis	3548(78)	1936	1936	1937	1937
HC Series 112 inch w/b	1938	Pick up	3548(85)	1937	1937	1938	1938
HC Series 112 inch w/b	1938	Chassis	3548(85)	1937	1937	1938	1938
SA Series 1½t 131 inch w/b	1938	Truck	3548(78)	1937	1937	1938	1938
SA Series 1½t 131 inch w/b	1938	Chassis	3548(78)	1937	1937	1938	1938
SB Series 1½t 131 inch w/b	1938	Truck	3548(78)	1937	1937	1938	1938
SB Series 1½t 131 inch w/b	1938	Chassis	3548(78)	1937	1937	1938	1938
SC Series 1½t 157 inch w/b	1938	Truck	3548(78)	1937	1937	1938	1938
SC Series 1½t 157 inch w/b	1938	Chassis	3548(78)	1937	1937	1938	1938
SD Series 1½t 157 inch w/b	1938	Truck	3548(78)	1937	1937	1938	1938
SD Series 1½t 157 inch w/b	1938	Chassis	3548(78)	1937	1937	1938	1938
JC Series 112 inch w/b	1939	Pick up	3548(85)	1938	1938	1940	1940
JC Series 112 inch w/b	1939	Chassis	3548(85)	1938	1938	1940	1940
TA Series 1½t 133 inch w/b	1939	Truck	3548(78)	1938	1938	1940	1940
TA Series 1½t 133 inch w/b	1939	Chassis	3548(78)	1938	1938	1940	1940
TB Series 1½t 133 inch w/b	1939	Truck	3548(78)	1938	1938	1940	1940
TB Series 1½t 133 inch w/b	1939	Chassis	3548(78)	1938	1938	1940	1940
TC Series 1½t 158½ inch	1939	Truck	3548(78)	1938	1938	1940	1940
TC Series 1½t 158½ inch	1939	Chassis	3548(78)	1938	1938	1940	1940
TD Series 1½t 158½ inch	1939	Truck	3548(78)	1938	1938	1940	1940
TD Series 1½t 158½ inch	1939	Chassis	3548(78)	1938	1938	1940	1940

General Motors Japan: Pontiac/Oldsmobile

Model group	General Motors Japan						
Final assembly:	Japan			Osaka			
Marque	Pontiac			Timeline			
Model	MY	Body type	Power unit	Intro.	Start	End	LOST
6 De Luxe	1935	Sedan 4dr	3408(80)	1935	1935	1935	1935
8	1935	Sedan 4dr	3661(84)	1935	1935	1935	1935
6 De Luxe	1936	Sedan 4dr	3408(80)	1935	1935	1936	1936
8	1936	Sedan 4dr	3807(87)	1935	1935	1936	1936
6 De Luxe	1937	Sedan 4dr	3649(85)	1936	1936	1937	1937
8	1937	Sedan 4dr	4079(100)	1936	1936	1937	1937
6 De Luxe	1938	Sedan 4dr	3649(85)	1937	1937	1938	1938
8	1938	Sedan 4dr	4079(100)	1937	1937	1938	1938
6 De Luxe	1939	Sedan 4dr	3649(85)	1938	1938	1939	1939
8	1939	Sedan 4dr	4079(100)	1938	1938	1939	1939

Model group	General Motors Japan						
Final assembly:	Japan			Osaka			
Marque	Oldsmobile			Timeline			
Model	MY	Body type	Power unit	Intro.	Start	End	LOST
6	1935	Sedan 4dr	3490(90)	1935	1935	1935	1935
8	1935	Sedan 4dr	3933(100)	1935	1935	1935	1935
6	1936	Sedan 4dr	3490(90)	1935	1935	1936	1936
8	1936	Sedan 4dr	3933(100)	1935	1935	1936	1936
6	1937	Sedan 4dr	3769(95)	1936	1936	1937	1937
8	1937	Sedan 4dr	4211(110)	1936	1936	1937	1937
6	1938	Sedan 4dr	3769(95)	1937	1937	1938	1938
8	1938	Sedan 4dr	4211(110)	1937	1937	1938	1938
6	1939	Sedan 4dr	3769(95)	1938	1938	1939	1939
8	1939	Sedan 4dr	4211(110)	1938	1938	1939	1939

General Motors models available in this period covered in previous volumes:
- Chevrolet DC Series Standard Six Sedan 2dr/4dr, 1934-1935, Volume 1
- Chevrolet DA Series Master Sedan 4dr/Coupe/Roadster, 1934-1935, Volume 1
- Chevrolet DB Series Half-Ton Van/Pick Up, 1934-1935, Volume 1
- Chevrolet PA/PB/PC/PD Series 1½t, 1934-1935, Volume 1
- Chevrolet P Series Utility Truck 2t, 1934-1935, Volume 1

General Motors, in common with the other American marques suffered declining popularity over the 1935-1939 period because of political interference. As with Ford, some model year 1939 models remained available until 1940. General Motor's lower volume marques (Buick, Cadillac, GMC) may also have been bulk assembled but insufficient evidence has been found to confirm this. These models would have been supplied built up or assembled to order.

General Motors Japan

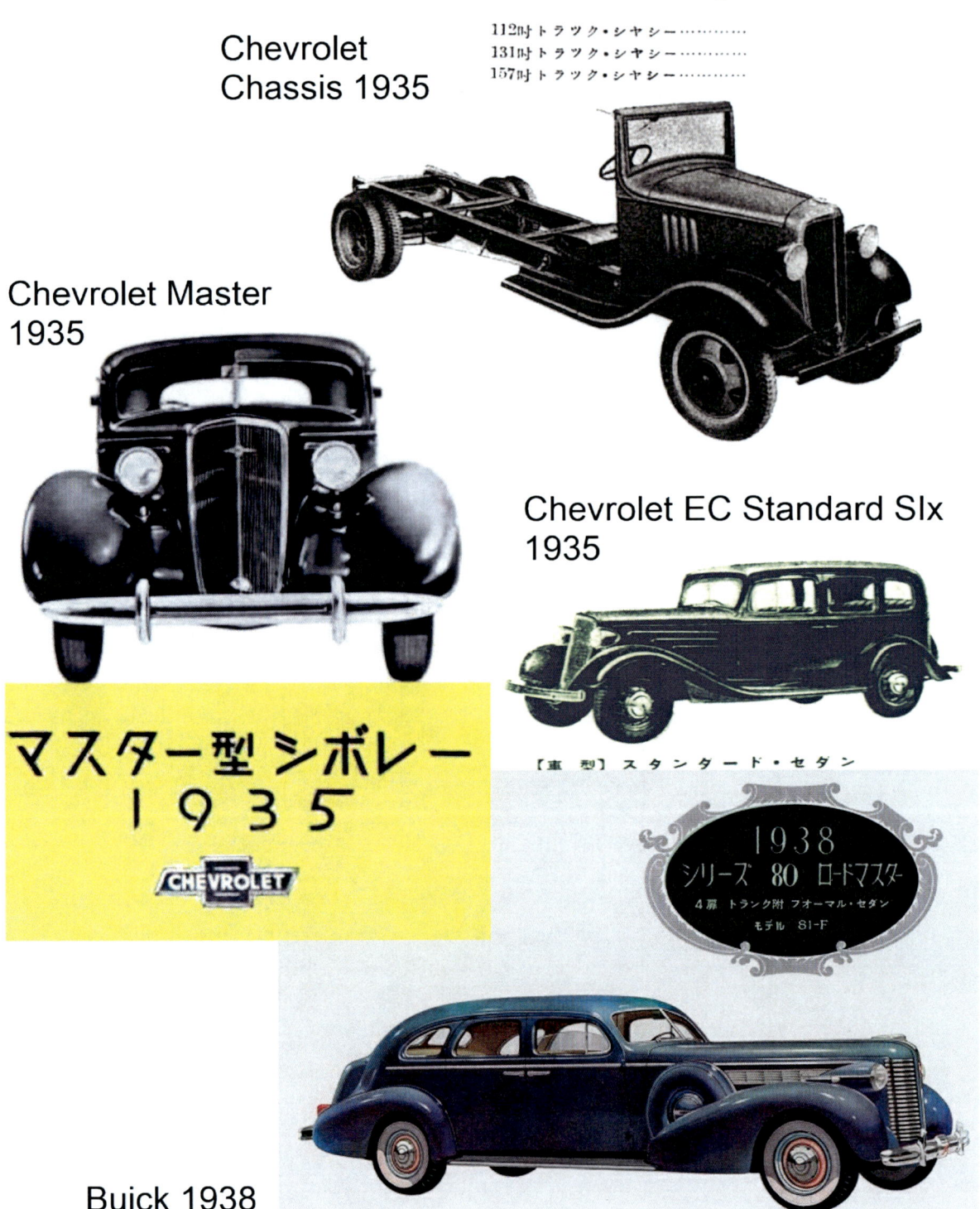

Chevrolet Chassis 1935

Chevrolet Master 1935

Chevrolet EC Standard SIx 1935

Buick 1938

Giant (Seiki Kogyo)

Model group	Giant NA							
Marque	Model							
Giant	NA							
Body type(s)	3 wheel cycle truck							
Power units	500	600			Timeline			
Final assembly:	Key market	Length (cm)		Drive	Intro.	Start	End	LOST
Japan	Japan			BMR	Circa 1935			
Variations: 5 (500cc), 6 (600cc)								

Model group	Giant NO							
Marque	Model							
Giant	NO							
Body type(s)	3 wheel cycle truck							
Power units	600				Timeline			
Final assembly:	Key market	Length (cm)		Drive	Intro.	Start	End	LOST
Japan	Japan			BMR	Circa 1935			

Model group	Giant KA							
Marque	Model							
Giant	KA							
Body type(s)	3 wheel cycle truck							
Power units	650	750			Timeline			
Final assembly:	Key market	Length (cm)		Drive	Intro.	Start	End	LOST
Japan	Japan			BMR	1935	1935	1937	1937
Variations: 6 (650cc), 7 (750cc)								

Model group	Giant Rex original							
Marque	Model							
Giant	REX							
Body type(s)	3 wheel cycle truck							
Power units	750				Timeline			
Final assembly:	Key market	Length (cm)		Drive	Intro.	Start	End	LOST
Japan	Japan			BMR	1935	1935	1937	1937

Model group	Giant Rex revised 1937							
Marque	Model							
Giant	REX							
Body type(s)	3 wheel cycle truck							
Power units	650	750			Timeline			
Final assembly:	Key market	Length (cm)		Drive	Intro.	Start	End	LOST
Japan	Japan			BMR	1937	1937	1940	1940
Variations: REX-1 (650), REX-2 (750)								

Giant

KA6 1936

Rex 1935

Rex 1 1937

One of the more prominent sanrinsha manufacturers. Giant later became the Cony brand. Rex, the newest model was replaced by the AA series starting in 1946.

Rex 2 1939

Harley Davidson

Models available in this period covered in previous volumes:
- RL Servicar, 1932-1937, Volume 1
- VL Servicar, 1932-1937, Volume 1
- VL Route Van, 1932-1937, Volume 1

Hijiri

Hijiri was a supplier to Ford that started making trucks similar to the Ford BB. Production continued into the 1940s but no evidence of any vehicles made post war.

Model group								
Marque		Hijiri original						
Hijiri		Model						
Body type(s)		Truck		Chassis				
Power units	3285(50)					Timeline		
Final assembly:		Key market	Length (cm)	Drive	Intro.	Start	End	LOST
Japan		Japan		FR	1935	1935	1939	1939
Variations: 1.5t, 1.8t, 2.0t								

Model group								
Marque		Hijiri revised 1939						
Hijiri		Model						
Body type(s)		Truck		Chassis				
Power units	3285(50)					Timeline		
Final assembly:		Key market	Length (cm)	Drive	Intro.	Start	End	LOST
Japan		Japan		FR	1939	1939	1942	1943
Variations: 1.5t, 1.8t, 2.0t								

Hirano (Hirano Seizakusho)

Model group								
Marque		Hirano						
Hirano		Model						
Body type(s)		3 wheel cycle truck		3 wheel cycle van				
Power units	674(7)					Timeline		
Final assembly:		Key market	Length (cm)	Drive	Intro.	Start	End	LOST
Japan	Nagoya	Japan		BMR	1936	1936	1940	1940

Hijiri

Hijiri Truck 1937

聖　號

Hijiri Chassis 1939

【車型】聖トラック

Hijiri Truck 1939

Hirano

Hirano Truck

Hitachi-Federal

American Federal trucks assembled in Japan in conjunction with Hitachi. Concentrated on larger trucks but also made the lower capacity models covered in this volume. Termination date of these models is unclear but thought to be around 1938.

Model group	\multicolumn{5}{c}{Hitachi-Federal}				
Marque				Model				
Hitachi-Federal				FE				
Body type(s)	Truck chassis							
Power units						Timeline		
Final assembly:		Key market	Length (cm)	Drive	Intro.	Start	End	LOST
Japan	Tokyo	Japan		FR	1934	1934	1938	1938
Variations: 15 (1.5t), 20 (2.0t)								

Model group				Hitachi-Federal				
Marque				Model				
Hitachi-Federal				B 15				
Body type(s)	Bus chassis							
Power units						Timeline		
Final assembly:		Key market	Length (cm)	Drive	Intro.	Start	End	LOST
Japan	Tokyo	Japan		FR	1934	1934	1938	1938

Hitakashi

Model group				Hitakashi				
Marque				Model				
Hitakashi				Go				
Body type(s)	Truck							
Power units						Timeline		
Final assembly:		Key market	Length (cm)	Drive	Intro.	Start	End	LOST
Japan		Japan				Circa 1939		

Hoxon

Model group				Hoxon				
Marque				Model				
Hoxon				660cc				
Body type(s)	3 wheel cycle truck							
Power units	660					Timeline		
Final assembly:		Key market	Length (cm)	Drive	Intro.	Start	End	LOST
Japan		Japan		BMR	1936	1936	1940	1940

Hitachi-Federal

B15 Chassis 1935

【車 型】 B 15型 バス・シヤシー

FE20 1935

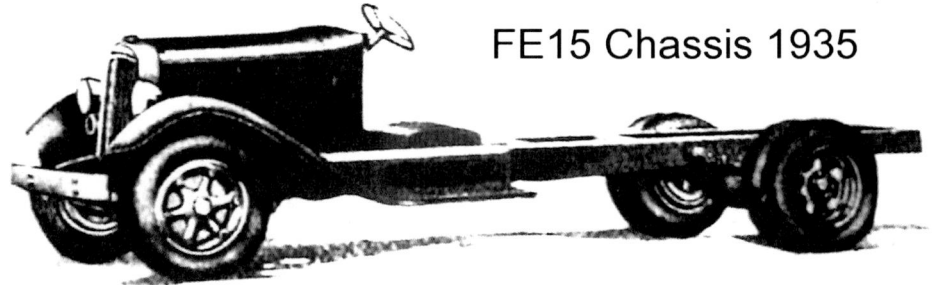

FE15 Chassis 1935

Hitakashi

Go 1939

Hyogo (HMC)

Motorbike manufacturer that moved into sanrinsha production but did not continue post war. Smaller engined models probably deleted around 1937/38. This entry covers later versions of models introduced in volume 1 of this book series.

Model group				Hyogo				
Marque				Model				
Hyogo				HMC3				
Body type(s)	3 wheel cycle truck							
Power units	600	650	744		Timeline			
Final assembly:		Key market	Length (cm)	Drive	Intro.	Start	End	LOST
Japan	Hyogo	Japan		BMR	1933	1933	1940	1940

Ikegai (Kawasaki Machinery Co)

This entry covers later versions of models introduced in volume 1 of this book series.

Model group				Ikegai				
Marque				Model				
Ikegai				FT				
Body type(s)	Truck chassis							
Power units	4396D(50/60)				Timeline			
Final assembly:		Key market	Length (cm)	Drive	Intro.	Start	End	LOST
Japan	Kawasaki	Japan		FR	1934	1934	1940	1940
Variations: 15 (1.5t), 20 (2.0t)								

Model group				Ikegai				
Marque				Model				
Ikegai				DT				
Body type(s)	Truck chassis							
Power units	6597D(70/90)				Timeline			
Final assembly:		Key market	Length (cm)	Drive	Intro.	Start	End	LOST
Japan	Kawasaki	Japan		FR	1934	1934	1940	1940
Variations: 15 (1.5t), 20 (2.0t)								

Model group				Ikegai				
Marque				Model				
Ikegai				DB20				
Body type(s)	Bus chassis							
Power units	6597D(70/90)				Timeline			
Final assembly:		Key market	Length (cm)	Drive	Intro.	Start	End	LOST
Japan	Kawasaki	Japan		FR	1934	1934	1940	1940

Hoxon

Go 660 1936

Go 660 1940

Hyogo

HMC3

DB 20

Ikegai

FT 15

Mainly larger capacity commercials manufactured. FT light duty models supplied in chassis form for truck and bus applications.

Heavy duty models were the DT (truck) and DB (bus) models.

Isuzu (Tokyo Automobile Industries Co)

Isuzu continued the TX35 and TX45 models into this period with modernisation revisions in 1937 including a new sloping front. Production from 1938 was at the new Kawasaki plant but some production of new models was at the old factory in Tokyo. An extended "Long" model was now available as well as a TX50 version of the Long with DA40 diesel engine. Type 94 production continues essentially unchanged over this period. Company becomes Tokyo Automobile Industries (as translated) from 1937 and trucks all have Isuzu badges from then, dropping the Sumida and Chiyoda marques.

Isuzu/Sumida/Chiyoda truck models available in this period covered in previous volumes:
- Sumida E33, 1934-1937, Volume 1
- Isuzu TX original, 1933-1937, Volume 1
- Isuzu BX original, 1933-1937, Volume 1
- Isuzu/Sumida/Chiyoda Type 94, 1934-1945, Volume 1(Sumida/Chiyoda to 1937)
- Chiyoda Model J, 1934-1937, Volume 1
- Sumida Model S, 1934-1937, Volume 1

Model group		Isuzu: Isuzu TX revised 1937; Isuzu Type 97 original						
Model sub group		Isuzu TX35						
Marque		Model						
Isuzu		TX35						
Body type(s)	Truck chassis	Truck						
Power units	4398(70)				Timeline			
Final assembly:		Key market	Length (cm)	Drive	Intro.	Start	End	LOST
Japan	Kawasaki	Japan	595 (truck)	FR	1937	1937	1945	1945

Model group		Isuzu: Isuzu TX revised 1937; Isuzu Type 97 original						
Model sub group		Isuzu TX40						
Marque		Model						
Isuzu		TX40						
Body type(s)	Truck chassis	Truck						
Power units	4398(70)				Timeline			
Final assembly:		Key market	Length (cm)	Drive	Intro.	Start	End	LOST
Japan	Kawasaki	Japan	595 (truck)	FR	1937	1937	1945	1945

Isuzu (Tokyo Automobile Industries Co)

Model group		Isuzu: Isuzu TX revised 1937; Isuzu Type 97 original						
Model sub group		Isuzu TX40						
Marque		Model						
Isuzu		TX40 long						
Body type(s)	Truck chassis	Truck						
Power units	4398(70)				Timeline			
Final assembly:		Key market	Length (cm)	Drive	Intro.	Start	End	LOST
Japan	Kawasaki	Japan	673 (truck)	FR	1937	1937	1945	1945

Model group		Isuzu: Isuzu TX revised 1937; Isuzu Type 97 original						
Model sub group		Isuzu TX50						
Marque		Model						
Isuzu		TX50						
Body type(s)	Truck chassis	Truck						
Power units	5100D(85)				Timeline			
Final assembly:		Key market	Length (cm)	Drive	Intro.	Start	End	LOST
Japan	Kawasaki	Japan	673 (truck)	FR	1940	1940	1945	1945

Model group		Isuzu: Isuzu TX revised 1937; Isuzu Type 97 original						
Model sub group		Isuzu Type 97						
Marque		Model						
Isuzu		Type 97						
Body type(s)	Truck chassis	Truck						
Power units	4398(70)				Timeline			
Final assembly:		Key market	Length (cm)	Drive	Intro.	Start	End	LOST
Japan	Kawasaki	Japan	673 (truck)	FR	1937	1938	1940	1940

Model group		Isuzu: Isuzu BX						
Model sub group		Isuzu BX						
Marque		Model						
Isuzu		BX						
Body type(s)	Bus chassis							
Power units	4398(70)				Timeline			
Final assembly:		Key market	Length (cm)	Drive	Intro.	Start	End	LOST
Japan	Kawasaki	Japan		FR	1937	1937	1945	1945
Variations: BX35, BX40								

Model group		Isuzu: Isuzu BX revised 1937						
Model sub group		Isuzu BX50						
Marque		Model						
Isuzu		BX50						
Body type(s)	Bus chassis							
Power units	5100D(85)				Timeline			
Final assembly:		Key market	Length (cm)	Drive	Intro.	Start	End	LOST
Japan	Kawasaki	Japan		FR	1940	1940	1945	1945

Isuzu

Military Type 94 continued production through and beyond the period covered by this volume. Remaining models on this page are post 1937 sloping front evolutions of the Isuzu truck series.

Type 94

TX35 Chassis

TX range brochure 1939

TX35 Chassis with Double Cab

Isuzu

TX40 1939

TX40 based Type 97 soft top cab 1937

TX40 chassis with ambulance bodywork 1939

TX40 Long 1939

Isuzu

BX40

BX40 (top)
TX40 (bottom)
Chassis

BX40
1941

BX40
1939

Isuzu: Chiyoda (Tokyo Gas and Electric)

Chiyoda was an Isuzu affiliated brand produced by Tokyo Gas and Electric (TGE). When TGE became fully absorbed into Tokyo Automobile Industries in 1937 the Chiyoda brand was dropped for both car and trucks. Chiyoda branded production cars and prototypes were still being produced until 1937. HA prototype is a copy of the 1936 Hudson and has therefore been included in this volume but some sources list this model as early as 1933.

> Chiyoda car models available in this period covered in previous volumes:
> - Chiyoda Model H, 1932-1937, Volume 1
> - Chiyoda Model HF, 1936-1937, Volume 1
> - Chiyoda Model HS, 1932-1936, Volume 1

Model group		Isuzu: Chiyoda H; Sumida H revised 1936						
Model sub group		Chiyoda HA						
Marque		Model						
Chiyoda		Model HA						
Body type(s)	Sedan 4dr							
Power units	4398(70)				Timeline			
Final assembly:		Key market	Length (cm)	Drive	Intro.	Start	End	LOST
Japan	Tokyo		520	FR	1936	P	P	P

Isuzu: Sumida (Jidosha Kogyo)

> Sumida car models available in this period covered in previous volumes:
> - Sumida Model H, 1933-1936, Volume 1(dates amended from volume one)
> - Sumida Model H (big body), 1933-1936, Volume 1(dates amended from volume one)
> - Sumida Model J, 1933-1937, Volume 1
> - Sumida Model K-93, 1933-1936, Volume 1

Model group		Isuzu: Chiyoda H; Sumida H revised 1936						
Model sub group		Sumida HB						
Marque		Model						
Sumida		Model HB						
Body type(s)	Sedan 4dr							
Power units	3410(60)				Timeline			
Final assembly:		Key market	Length (cm)	Drive	Intro.	Start	End	LOST
Japan	Tokyo	Japan	520	FR	1936	1936	1937	1937

Isuzu: Chiyoda

1936 HF was a four wheel drive version of H Phaeton. Front style resembled six wheel HS with a slope to the radiator and side vents.

HF

HA

Isuzu: Sumida

Hudson look alike models did not get beyond prototype stage and use the X engine (Chiyoda HA) or a 3.4l unit (Sumida HB).

HB

Isuzu: Sumida (Jidosha Kogyo)

Following the 1937 company re-organisation the Sumida name plate was dropped from truck models as previously stated. Production details from this period are confusing and contradictory but the Sumida badge appears to have continued on cars produced by Tokyo Automobile Industries until the beginning of the 1940s when all remaining models were modified and re-named as Isuzu products. Existing sedan production was discontinued around 1937 and the prototype sedan models were not developed. Civilian production, which was very limited anyway, also discontinued around this time. Revised phaeton models continued in production for military use only.

Prior to the 1937 discontinuation there were some developments to existing models however: the H was modified in 1936 to receive the new C6A air cooled power unit to create the HA and its HD "Big Body" equivalent. There was also an HE model, details are unclear but this is thought to have been an HD with a prototype V8. Side view illustrations in this volume show the H and subsequent HA model to be virtually identical. HD was intended as more of a limousine and uses the same shell as the H "Big Body" with its split windscreen style. The side view illustrates the rounded aeroplane style windows, rear coach doors and external boot.

Petrol phaeton models all use the old 70hp X engine. The HA Phaeton is a civilian version of the J model with revised styling. It is unclear if any were made as only artist impressions have been found of this model. The Sumida JC is a development of the Sumida J with four wheel drive, the JD model being the diesel equivalent. The K10 is a modified 6x4 K-93 with a sloping front. These military models were replaced by similar Isuzu K and KP models in 1940-41.

Model group	Isuzu: Chiyoda H; Sumida H revised 1936							
Model sub group	Sumida HA							
Marque	Model							
Sumida	Model HA							
Body type(s)	Sedan 4dr							
Power units	4580(75)				Timeline			
Final assembly:		Key market	Length (cm)	Drive	Intro.	Start	End	LOST
Japan	Tokyo	Japan		FR	1936	1936	1937	1937

Model group	Isuzu: Chiyoda H; Sumida H revised 1936							
Model sub group	Sumida HD							
Marque	Model							
Sumida	Model HD							
Body type(s)	Sedan 4dr							
Power units	4580(75)				Timeline			
Final assembly:		Key market	Length (cm)	Drive	Intro.	Start	End	LOST
Japan	Tokyo	Japan		FR	1936	1936	1937	1937

Isuzu: Sumida (Jidosha Kogyo)

Model group		Isuzu: Chiyoda H; Sumida H revised 1936						
Model sub group		Sumida HE						
Marque		Model						
Sumida		Model HE						
Body type(s)	Sedan 4dr							
Power units	V8				Timeline			
Final assembly:		Key market	Length (cm)	Drive	Intro.	Start	End	LOST
Japan	Tokyo	Japan		FR	1936	1936	1937	1937

Model group		Isuzu: Chiyoda H; Sumida H revised 1936						
Model sub group		Sumida HA Phaeton						
Marque		Model						
Sumida		Model HA						
Body type(s)	Phaeton 4dr							
Power units	4398(70)				Timeline			
Final assembly:		Key market	Length (cm)	Drive	Intro.	Start	End	LOST
Japan	Tokyo	Japan		FR	1936	1936	1937	1937

Model group		Isuzu: Sumida J; Sumida K; Isuzu K; Isuzu PK revised 1937						
Model sub group		Sumida Type 98 original						
Marque		Model						
Sumida		Model JC Type 98 KIJI A Phaeton 4dr						
Body type(s)	Phaeton 4dr							
Power units	4398(70)				Timeline			
Final assembly:		Key market	Length (cm)	Drive	Intro.	Start	End	LOST
Japan	Kawasaki	Japan	495	F4	1937	1937	1940	1940

Model group		Isuzu: Sumida J; Sumida K; Isuzu K; Isuzu PK revised 1937						
Model sub group		Sumida Type 98 original						
Marque		Model						
Sumida		Model JD Type 98 KIJI B Phaeton 4dr						
Body type(s)	Phaeton 4dr							
Power units	4200D(70)				Timeline			
Final assembly:		Key market	Length (cm)	Drive	Intro.	Start	End	LOST
Japan	Kawasaki	Japan	495	F4	1937	1937	1940	1940

Model group		Isuzu: Sumida J; Sumida K; Isuzu K; Isuzu PK revised 1937						
Model sub group		Sumida K-10						
Marque		Model						
Sumida		Model K10 Type 96 Phaeton						
Body type(s)	Phaeton 2dr 6w							
Power units	4398(70)				Timeline			
Final assembly:		Key market	Length (cm)	Drive	Intro.	Start	End	LOST
Japan	Kawasaki	Japan	518	F6x4	1937	1937	1940	1940

Isuzu: Sumida

H

HA

HD

K-10

Isuzu: Sumida

HA Phaeton is a civilian version of the military staff car Model J. The H Phaeton has more elaborate wheels, wings and side vents and added horns but loses the side mounted wheel.

J Phaeton

HA Phaeton

Type 98 JC and JD

Iwasaki (Asahi Nainenki)

This section contains model information updated from Pomchi Volume 1 and includes additional information on models from the period covered in that volume.

IMC models are water cooled, KMK air cooled.

Model group				Iwasaki				
Marque				Model				
Iwasaki				IMC 650				
Body type(s)	3 wheel cycle truck							
Power units	650				Timeline			
Final assembly:		Key market	Length (cm)	Drive	Intro.	Start	End	LOST
Japan	Osaka	Japan		BMR	1932	1932	1935	1935

Model group				Iwasaki				
Marque				Model				
Iwasaki				KMK 650				
Body type(s)	5 wheel cycle truck							
Power units	650				Timeline			
Final assembly:		Key market	Length (cm)	Drive	Intro.	Start	End	LOST
Japan	Osaka	Japan		BMR	1932	1932	1935	1935

Model group				Iwasaki				
Marque				Model				
Iwasaki				IMC 750				
Body type(s)	4 wheel cycle truck							
Power units	750				Timeline			
Final assembly:		Key market	Length (cm)	Drive	Intro.	Start	End	LOST
Japan	Osaka	Japan		BMR	1934	1934	1942	1942

Model group				Iwasaki				
Marque				Model				
Iwasaki				1200cc				
Body type(s)	3 wheel cycle truck							
Power units	1200				Timeline			
Final assembly:		Key market	Length (cm)	Drive	Intro.	Start	End	LOST
Japan	Osaka	Japan		BMR	1939	1939	1942	1942

Model group				Iwasaki				
Marque				Model				
Iwasaki				ANK Sedan				
Body type(s)	3 wheel truck							
Power units	750				Timeline			
Final assembly:		Key market	Length (cm)	Drive	Intro.	Start	End	LOST
Japan	Osaka	Japan		FR	1938	1938	1942	1942

Iwasaki

IWC 1936

 1940

1200cc

 ANK

JAC

JAC is a 6 cylinder Chrysler copy. Details are limited but it may have used leftover Chrysler parts in locally administered production facility. Nihon Nainenki (New Era/Kurogane) also made products under the JAC name but it is not clear if these cars are connected.

Model group		J.A.C.					
Marque		Model					
J.A.C.		Sedan					
Body type(s)	Saloon 4dr						
Power units	3670				Timeline		
Final assembly:		Key market	Length (cm)	Drive	Intro.	Start	End	LOST
Japan		Japan		FR	1939	1939	1940	1940

Kokueki

Limited information, estimated dates.

Model group		Kokueki					
Marque		Model					
Kokueki							
Body type(s)	3 wheel cycle truck						
Power units	622				Timeline		
Final assembly:		Key market	Length (cm)	Drive	Intro.	Start	End	LOST
Japan		Japan		BMR	1937	1937	1939	1939

Model group		Kokueki					
Marque		Model					
Kokueki							
Body type(s)	Truck						
Power units	722				Timeline		
Final assembly:		Key market	Length (cm)	Drive	Intro.	Start	End	LOST
Japan		Japan		BMR	1937	1937	1939	1939

Kurakawa

Included because of listing in Georgano encyclopaedia but no other trace found. Production figure of 2,050 is identical to that listed for Kyosan but no connection has been established.

Model group		Kurakawa					
Marque		Model					
Kurakawa							
Body type(s)	3 wheel cycle truck						
Power units	650				Timeline		
Final assembly:		Key market	Length (cm)	Drive	Intro.	Start	End	LOST
Japan		Japan		BMR	1937	1937	1937	1937

JAC

J．A．C－特殊型

Kokueki

722cc

650cc Truck

Kurogane: New Era (Nihon Jidosha)

Model group	Kurogane Model 1, New Era							
Model sub group	New Era revised 1935							
Marque	Model							
New Era	650cc							
Body type(s)	3 wheel cycle truck								
Power units	649(15.5)	747(16)				Timeline			
Final assembly:		Key market	Length (cm)		Drive	Intro.	Start	End	LOST
Japan	Tokyo	Japan			BMR	1935	1935	1937	1937

Kurogane (Nihon Nainenki)

The New Era marque became Kurogane (Black Metal) over this period. Kurogane Model 1 was used in significant numbers by the military. It is unclear if the people carrier versions shown were factory supplied - various taxi versions were available with minor styling differences. The Model 1 re-entered limited production for a short period after the Second World War before being replaced in 1950 with a new range of three wheelers.

Model group	Kurogane Model 1, New Era								
Model sub group	Kurogane Model 1								
Marque	Model								
Kurogane	Model 1 650cc								
Body type(s)	3 wheel cycle truck								
Power units	747(16.5)					Timeline			
Final assembly:		Key market	Length (cm)	Drive		Intro.	Start	End	LOST
Japan	Tokyo	Japan	280	BMR		1937	1937	1940	1940

Model group	Kurogane Model 1, New Era								
Model sub group	Kurogane Model 1								
Marque	Model								
Kurogane	Model 1 750cc								
Body type(s)	3 wheel cycle truck		Military Passenger		Taxi				
Power units	747(16.5)					Timeline			
Final assembly:		Key market	Length (cm)	Drive		Intro.	Start	End	LOST
Japan	Tokyo	Japan	280	BMR		1937	1937	1944	1944

Model group	Kurogane Model 1, New Era								
Model sub group	Kurogane Model 1 1200cc								
Marque	Model								
Kurogane	Model 1								
Body type(s)	3 wheel cycle truck								
Power units	1196(22)					Timeline			
Final assembly:		Key market	Length (cm)	Drive		Intro.	Start	End	LOST
Japan	Tokyo	Japan		BMR		1937	1937	1944	1944

Kurogane/New Era

New Era 650cc
1936

Kurogane Model 1
1937

Kurogane Model 1
1939

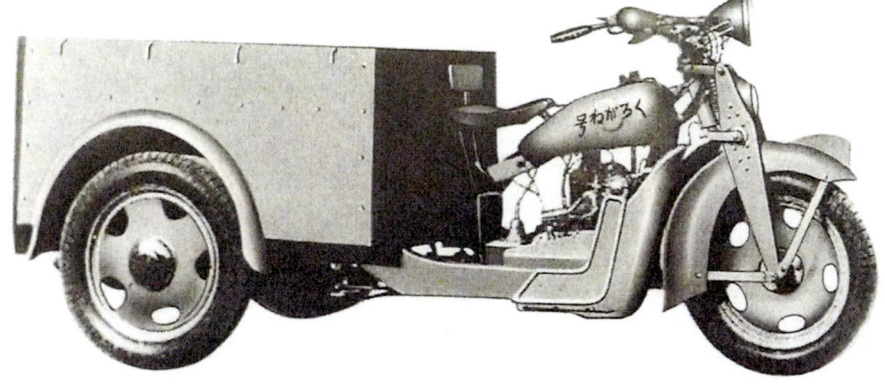

Kurogane

Kurogane Model 1 (left), Model 1 1200cc (right)

Kurogane Model 1 Military Pasenger

Kurogane Model 1 Taxi

Kurogane (Nihon Nainenki)

The Kurogane 95 was available in a number of different versions with bodies built by Yanase. Model 1 was a sedan believed to be a one-off with front wheel drive, independent front suspension and overhead valves.

Model 2 was a roadster style scout car prototype produced in a series of 10 units. It was similar mechanically to the sedan but fitted with a larger 1300cc engine. Seating was for four people – two inside, two using a dickey seat.

In 1934 the Japanese Imperial Army decided to develop a small scout car for reconnaissance work. A number of companies built prototypes including Kurogane who were asked to cooperate with the Toyoda and Okamoto companies to develop a prototype. This became the Type 95 Model 3, the most familiar of the Type 95 variants. This four wheel drive scout car of roadster configuration was extensively used by the military following its selection as the official product.

Power was from an air cooled (avoiding water availability issues) V-twin that developed 33 hp with capacity increased again over previous models to 1399cc. It also featured 4wd driven by a 3 speed manual gearbox as well as drum brakes, independent double wishbone front suspension with a semi-elliptical leaf spring suspended rear. Chassis was ladder frame and the simple bodywork could seat 2, or on later models 3 (2 front/1back). Engine and drive technology was developed by Tetsuji/Tetsushi Makita who also worked on the earlier Otomo car. Fuel consumption was in the thirties miles per gallon and the maximum speed 47mph.

Production of all types is given at 4,775 units. This includes Model 4 and Model 5 versions introduced in the 1940s that will be covered in the next Pomchi volume. The 4 door open prototype was not given a model reference.

A number of other companies vying for the military supply contract produced similar themed prototypes in roadster or phaeton configurations. All those identified have been included in this book series.

Model group				Kurogane Type 95			
Marque				Model			
Kurogane				Type 95 Model 1 Sedan 2dr			
Body type(s)	Sedan 2dr						
Power units	1196(22)				Timeline		
Final assembly:		Key market	Length (cm)	Drive	Intro.	Start	End	LOST
Japan	Tokyo			F4	1935	P	P	P

Kurogane

Type 95 Model 1

Type 95

Type 95 Model 2

Kurogane

Type 95

Type 95 Model 3

Type 95 Phaeton prototype

Kurogane (Nihon Nainenki)

Model group		Kurogane Type 95						
Marque		Model						
Kurogane		Type 95 Model 2 Roadster						
Body type(s)	Roadster							
Power units	1300				Timeline			
Final assembly:		Key market	Length (cm)	Drive	Intro.	Start	End	LOST
Japan	Tokyo		350	F4	1936	P	1937	P

Model group		Kurogane Type 95						
Marque		Model						
Kurogane		Type 95 Model 3 Staff Car						
Body type(s)	Roadster							
Power units	1399(33)				Timeline			
Final assembly:		Key market	Length (cm)	Drive	Intro.	Start	End	LOST
Japan	Tokyo	Japan	338	F4	1937	1937	1940	1940

Model group		Kurogane Type 95						
Marque		Model						
Kurogane		Type 95 Phaeton 4dr						
Body type(s)	Phaeton 4dr							
Power units	1399(33)				Timeline			
Final assembly:		Key market	Length (cm)	Drive	Intro.	Start	End	LOST
Japan	Tokyo			F4	1939	P	1939	P

Kyoho

Sanrinsha produced by cycle maker. No images are available for this model.

Model group		Kyoho						
Marque		Model						
Kyoho								
Body type(s)	3 wheel cycle truck							
Power units					Timeline			
Final assembly:		Key market	Length (cm)	Drive	Intro.	Start	End	LOST
Japan		Japan		BMR	1937	1937	1939	1939

Kyosan (Kyosan Electric Manufacturing Co)

Kyosan developed and refined their small truck ideas into the TB which was continually updated over the period it was available. They also made an unusual Flat Nose forward control version. Total production has been stated at 2,050 units.

Model group					Kyosan			
Marque					Model			
Kyosan					Go TB			
Body type(s)		Pick Up						
Power units		748(13)				Timeline		
Final assembly:		Key market	Length (cm)	Drive	Intro.	Start	End	LOST
Japan	Tokyo	Japan	280	FR	1936	1936	1937	1937

Model group					Kyosan			
Marque					Model			
Kyosan					Go TB			
Body type(s)		Pick Up						
Power units		748(13)				Timeline		
Final assembly:		Key market	Length (cm)	Drive	Intro.	Start	End	LOST
Japan	Tokyo	Japan	280	FR	1937	1937	1938	1938

Model group					Kyosan			
Marque					Model			
Kyosan					Go TB			
Body type(s)		Pick Up						
Power units		748(13)				Timeline		
Final assembly:		Key market	Length (cm)	Drive	Intro.	Start	End	LOST
Japan	Tokyo	Japan	280	FR	1938	1938	1939	1939

Model group					Kyosan			
Marque					Model			
Kyosan					Go Flat Nose			
Body type(s)		Pick Up						
Power units		748(13)				Timeline		
Final assembly:		Key market	Length (cm)	Drive	Intro.	Start	End	LOST
Japan	Tokyo	Japan		FR	1935	1935	1939	1939

Kyosan model available in this period covered in previous volumes:
- Go KB, 1932-1936, Volume 1

Kyosan

Go KB
1936

Kyosan

Go KB

Noticeably changed from 1936 model, 1937 version has D shaped bonnet vents, those on 1938 model are banana shaped.

Go KB 1937

Go KB 1938

Kyosan

Flat Nose

Matsuo

Examples of Matsuo limited production electric vehicles.

Coupe

Truck

Matsuo

Model group	Matsuo							
Marque	Model							
Matsuo								
Body type(s)	Coupe		Truck					
Power units	E					Timeline		
Final assembly:	Key market	Length (cm)	Drive	Intro.	Start	End	LOST	
Japan	Japan	280		Circa 1938				

Mazda (Matsuda)

These models are technically Matsuda Mazda products but were better known under the Mazda name and positioned in this volume as such. The KB model is an updated version of the previous KA, the KC and KE are further updates on the same theme. TCS combines the newer K series engine with frame from the old DC model. COP passenger model is KC based. GA starts a new model series with higher 0.5t load capacity. This model was reintroduced after the Second World War and remained available until 1949. Mazda, also experimented with four wheels at this time with a small sedan prototype, but four wheel vehicles were not pursued further until a few years after the end of the war.

Matsuda Mazda models available in this period covered in previous volumes:
- Go-DC, 1934-1935, Volume 1
- Go-KA, 1934-1935, Volume 1

Model group	Matsuda Mazda 3-wheeler (02) revised 1935 K-series,TCS, COP							
Model sub group	Mazda Go-KB							
Marque	Model							
Matsuda	Mazda Go-KB							
Body type(s)	3 wheel cycle truck							
Power units	654(13)					Timeline		
Final assembly:	Key market	Length (cm)	Drive	Intro.	Start	End	LOST	
Japan	Hiroshima	Japan	280	BMR	1935	1935	1935	1935

Model group	Matsuda Mazda 3-wheeler (02) revised 1935 K-series,TCS, COP							
Model sub group	Mazda Go-TCS							
Marque	Model							
Matsuda	Mazda Go-TCS							
Body type(s)	3 wheel cycle truck							
Power units	654(13)					Timeline		
Final assembly:	Key market	Length (cm)	Drive	Intro.	Start	End	LOST	
Japan	Hiroshima	Japan	280	BMR	1935	1935	1935	1935

Mazda

⇧

Mazda Go-TCS ⇨

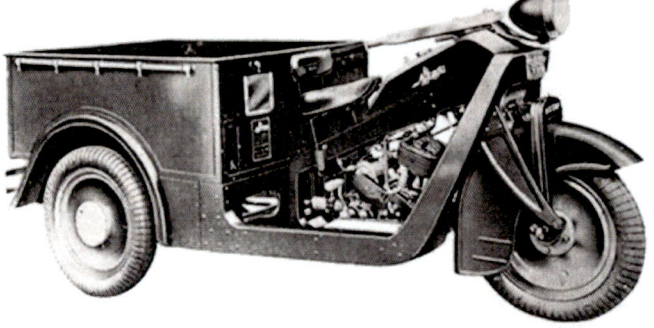

Mazda Go-KC 1936

Mazda Go-KC 1935

Mazda

Mazda Go-COP

Mazda Go-KE

Mazda GA

Mazda (Matsuda)

Model group		Matsuda Mazda 3-wheeler (02) revised 1935 K-series, TCS, COP						
Model sub group		Mazda Go-COP						
Marque		Model						
Matsuda		Mazda Go-COP						
Body type(s)	3 wheel cycle truck							
Power units	654(13)				Timeline			
Final assembly:		Key market	Length (cm)	Drive	Intro.	Start	End	LOST
Japan	Hiroshima	Japan	280	BMR	1936	1936	1938	1938

Model group		Matsuda Mazda 3-wheeler (02) revised 1935 K-series, TCS, COP						
Model sub group		Mazda Go-KC						
Marque		Model						
Matsuda		Mazda Go-KC						
Body type(s)	3 wheel cycle truck							
Power units	654(13)				Timeline			
Final assembly:		Key market	Length (cm)	Drive	Intro.	Start	End	LOST
Japan	Hiroshima	Japan	280	BMR	1935	1935	1936	1936

Model group		Matsuda Mazda 3-wheeler (02) revised 1935 K-series, TCS, COP						
Model sub group		Mazda Go-KE						
Marque		Model						
Matsuda		Mazda Go-KE36						
Body type(s)	3 wheel cycle truck							
Power units	654(13)				Timeline			
Final assembly:		Key market	Length (cm)	Drive	Intro.	Start	End	LOST
Japan	Hiroshima	Japan	280	BMR	1936	1936	1938	1938

Model group		Mazda 3-wheeler (03) G-series original						
Model sub group		Mazda GA						
Marque		Model						
Matsuda		Mazda GA						
Body type(s)	3 wheel cycle truck							
Power units	669(14)				Timeline			
Final assembly:		Key market	Length (cm)	Drive	Intro.	Start	End	LOST
Japan	Hiroshima	Japan	280	BMR	1938	1938	1945	1945

Model group		Mazda prototype 1939						
Marque		Model						
Mazda		Sedan						
Body type(s)	Sedan 2dr							
Power units					Timeline			
Final assembly:		Key market	Length (cm)	Drive	Intro.	Start	End	LOST
Japan	Hiroshima			FR	1939	P	1940	P

Mazda

Sedan prototype 1939

Mazda's first attempt at a proper car, as opposed to rickshaw versions of its truck models, was the small sedan illustrated. Details are limited and dates conflict but it seems likely a few were made over the period 1939-1940.

Mitsubishi (Mitsubishi Heavy Industries)

TD35 was the first commercially available diesel truck in Japan. As well as this 2t capacity model there was also a higher capacity TD45 model. Production was limited and there may have been some 4x4 versions for military use but this is unconfirmed. Mitsubishi also produced some of the Type 94 models more commonly known under Isuzu group badges. Production was limited to around 75 units with these models being discontinued when efforts turned to the TD series. Production switched to Tokyo in 1937 and the TD35 remained available until replaced by the also limited volume YB40 model in 1941.

Model group			Mitsubishi					
Marque			Model					
Mitsubishi			TD35					
Body type(s)		Truck						
Power units	6700D(70)					Timeline		
Final assembly:		Key market	Length (cm)		Drive	Intro.	Start	End	LOST
Japan	Kobe/Tokyo	Japan			FR	1936	1936	1941	1941

Mitsubishi models available in this period covered in previous volumes:
- Type 94, 1934-1936, Volume 1
- TSS-28, 1934-1936, Volume 1

Miyata (Miyata Works)

Small truck made by the same company as the Asahi car.

Model group			Miyata					
Marque			Model					
Miyata								
Body type(s)		Truck						
Power units						Timeline		
Final assembly:		Key market	Length (cm)		Drive	Intro.	Start	End	LOST
Japan	Tokyo					1937	1937	1939	1939

Mizuno Metal Works

The curious Mizuno continued to be available until 1940.

Mizuno model available in this period covered in previous volumes:
- Mizuno-shiki, 1925-1940, Volume 1

Mitsubishi

TD35

Miyata

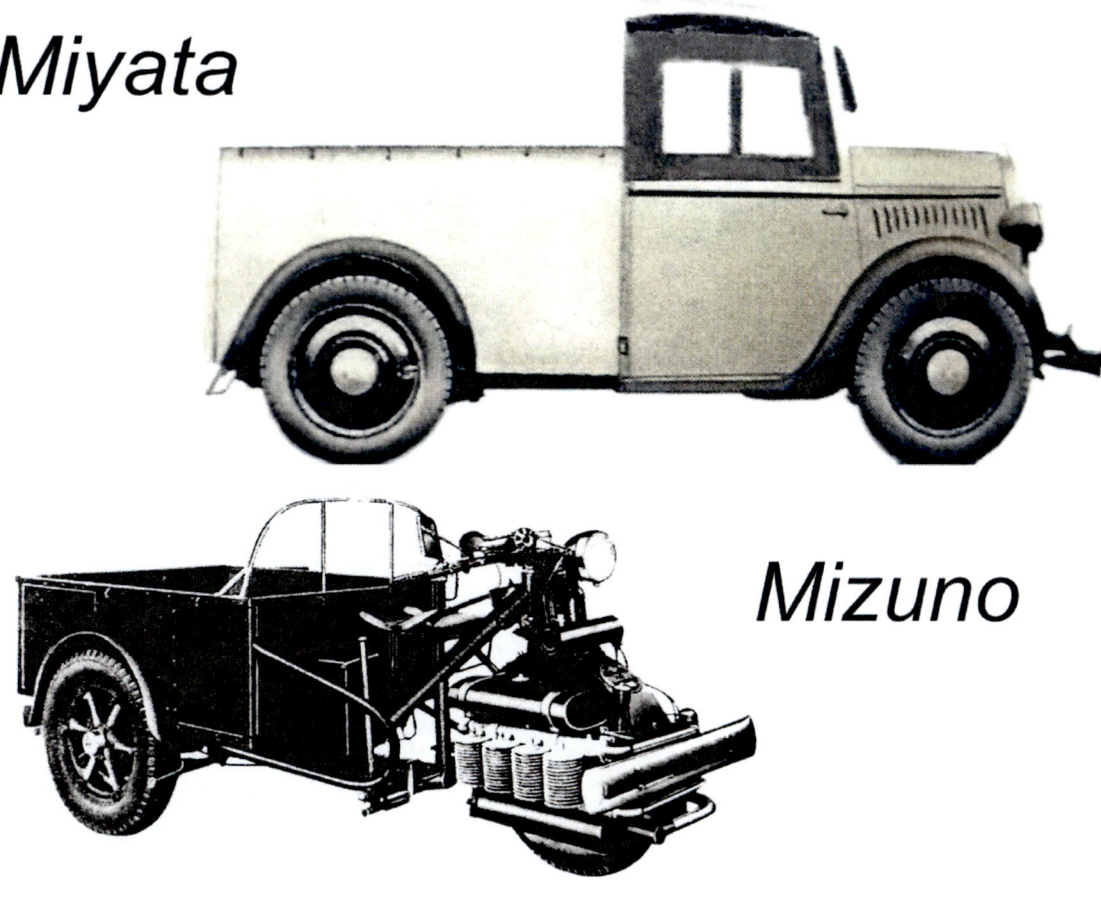

Mizuno

MSA

> MSA models available in this period covered in previous volumes:
> - MSA 3 400/500/650/675, 1930-1938, Volume 1
>
> (models listed may not have been available in all years)

Model group		MSA						
Marque		Model						
MSA		3						
Body type(s)	3 wheel cycle truck							
Power units	750				Timeline			
Final assembly:		Key market	Length (cm)	Drive	Intro.	Start	End	LOST
Japan	Tokyo	Japan		BMR	1935	1935	1938	1938

Nagoya (Nagoya Automotive Works)

Limited production electric vehicles with car or truck bodywork.

Model group		Nagoya						
Marque		Model						
Nagoya		Sedan						
Body type(s)	Sedan 4dr		Truck					
Power units	E				Timeline			
Final assembly:		Key market	Length (cm)	Drive	Intro.	Start	End	LOST
Japan	Nagoya	Japan			1939	1939	1939	1939

Nakajima (Nakajima Seisakusho/Yuasa Battery)

Another company producing small numbers of electric vehicles in sedan, truck and van varieties. Production of these vehicles was subsidised by the Ministry of Commerce and Industry.

Model group		Nakajima						
Marque		Model						
Nakajima		Sedan						
Body type(s)	Sedan 2dr							
Power units	E				Timeline			
Final assembly:		Key market	Length (cm)	Drive	Intro.	Start	End	LOST
Japan		Japan			1937	1937	1938	1938

MSA

3 650cc 1935

3 675cc 1937

Nagoya

Electric sedan

Nagoya

Electric truck

Nakajima

Electric truck

Electric sedan

Electric van

Nakajima (Nakajima Seisakusho/Yuasa Battery)

Model group		Nakajima						
Marque		Model						
Nakajima								
Body type(s)		Van		Truck				
Power units		E				Timeline		
Final assembly:		Key market	Length (cm)		Drive	Intro.	Start	End	LOST
Japan		Japan				1938	1938	1940	1940

Nichiden (NEC Automotive Works)

Model group		Nichiden						
Marque		Model						
Nichiden		Electric truck						
Body type(s)		Truck						
Power units		E				Timeline		
Final assembly:		Key market	Length (cm)		Drive	Intro.	Start	End	LOST
Japan		Japan				Circa 1937			

Nikko

The six cylinder model is a 1938 Dodge copy with different trim details. Four cylinder model is a short version of the six cylinder model with no Dodge equivalent. Limited information available but these may have used leftover Chrysler parts put together in a locally administered facility. JAC marque is also a leftover Chrysler design that may have been produced on this basis.

Model group		Nikko						
Marque		Model						
Nikko		4						
Body type(s)	Sedan 4dr							
Power units	2199(48)					Timeline		
Final assembly:		Key market	Length (cm)		Drive	Intro.	Start	End	LOST
Japan		Japan	420		FR	1939	1939	1940	1940

Model group		Nikko						
Marque		Model						
Nikko		6						
Body type(s)	Sedan 4dr							
Power units	3612(90)					Timeline		
Final assembly:		Key market	Length (cm)		Drive	Intro.	Start	End	LOST
Japan		Japan			FR	1939	1939	1940	1940

Nichiden

Electric truck

Nikko

4 cylinder

6 cylinder

Nissan: Datsun (Nissan Motor Co)

> Nissan: Datsun model available in this period covered in previous volumes:
>
> - Type 13, 1934-1935, Volume 1

Type 14

Nissan's small car offering that was available in a wide range of different body styles. Type 14 models have similar appearance to earlier Type 13 but gain a leaping rabbit mascot, although this isn't always fitted in corporate images. Mechanically a new engine sees a capacity drop to 722cc but power increased to 15hp.

Sedan, Phaeton and Roadster varieties continue in similar form to the Type 13. Phaeton and Roadster models now have forward opening coach doors

Route Vans were available in Panel format with twin rear doors, or as a Window model with single rear door and saloon like styling. Type 15/17 vans feature the slanted bonnet side vents of other commercial models.

Truck models in the Type 14/15 series were available as either a hard top Type B or a soft top Type A. The Type A style has only been traced to these models but may have been available on other types. Chassis models were available with the previous flat front grille or the sloping style.

Model group	Nissan: Datson/Datsun Type 10 to Type 17 revised 1935 Type 14							
Model sub group	Datsun Type 14							
Marque	Model							
Datsun	Type 14							
Body type(s)	Sedan 2dr		Phaeton 2dr		Roadster			
	Route Van Panel		Route Van Window					
Power units	722(15)						Timeline	
Final assembly:		Key market	Length (cm)	Drive	Intro.	Start	End	LOST
Japan	Yokohama	Japan	280	FR	1935	1935	1936	1936

Model group	Nissan: Datson/Datsun Type 10 to Type 17 revised 1935 Type 14							
Model sub group	Datsun Type 14							
Marque	Model							
Datsun	Type 14-T							
Body type(s)	Truck Type A		Truck Type B		Chassis			
Power units	722(15)						Timeline	
Final assembly:		Key market	Length (cm)	Drive	Intro.	Start	End	LOST
Japan	Yokohama	Japan	280	FR	1935	1935	1936	1936

Nissan:Datsun

13 Sedan

Type 14 brochure

Datsun
Type 13/14

14 Sedan

Nissan:Datsun

Datsun Type 14

14 Roadster

14 Phaeton

Nissan:Datsun

14 Route Van Panel

Window Route Van has car like styling.

Datsun Type 14

14 Route Van Window

14-T Truck Type A

Fabric top/half door

Metal top/ full door

14-T Truck Type B

Nissan: Datsun (Nissan Motor Co)

Type 15

Type 15 models received a longer body allowing more space and opted for a more upright frontal look that was generally considered to be less attractive than the previous model. Non-commercial models featured bonnet side vents with centrally placed chrome strips. Van and truck models retained the slanting slots of the type 14. Power unit was the same as for the Type 14 but now with slightly more (16 hp) power. Body styles remained the same as previously and the coupe model also made a return. This was initially a 3 window as on the last available Type 12 but there was also a 5 window version with small almost triangular back windows (see picture in Type 15 section). The coupe models were built in limited numbers and may not have got beyond prototype production stage but the 5 window theme was adopted for the following Type 16 model. The roadster is now called the Road-Star. An optional wide finishing strip for the grill centre was available, similar to that adopted on all Type 17 models.

Model group	Nissan: Datson/Datsun Type 10 to Type 17 revised 1936 Type 15							
Model sub group	Datsun Type 15							
Marque	Model							
Datsun	Type 15							
Body type(s)	Sedan 2dr		Coupe 3 window		Coupe 5 window			
	Phaeton 2dr							
Power units	722(16)					Timeline			
Final assembly:		Key market	Length (cm)	Drive	Intro.	Start	End	LOST
Japan	Yokohama	Japan	319	FR	1936	1936	1937	1937

Model group	Nissan: Datson/Datsun Type 10 to Type 17 revised 1936 Type 15							
Model sub group	Datsun Type 15							
Marque	Model							
Datsun	Type 15 Road-Star							
Body type(s)	Roadster							
Power units	722(16)					Timeline			
Final assembly:		Key market	Length (cm)	Drive	Intro.	Start	End	LOST
Japan	Yokohama	Japan	319	FR	1936	1936	1937	1937

Model group	Nissan: Datson/Datsun Type 10 to Type 17 revised 1936 Type 15							
Model sub group	Datsun Type 15							
Marque	Model							
Datsun	Type 15 Route Van							
Body type(s)	Panel		Window					
Power units	722(16)					Timeline			
Final assembly:		Key market	Length (cm)	Drive	Intro.	Start	End	LOST
Japan	Yokohama	Japan	319	FR	1936	1936	1938	1938

Nissan:Datsun

Datsun Type 15 Sedan

Nissan:Datsun

Datsun Type 15

15 Coupe 3 window

15 Coupe 5 window

15 Phaeton

Nissan:Datsun

15 Road-Star

Datsun Type 15

15 Road-Star

15 Route Van (Panel)

Nissan:Datsun

Datsun
Type 15-T

Nissan: Datsun (Nissan Motor Co)

Model group	Nissan: Datson/Datsun Type 10 to Type 17 revised 1936 Type 15						
Model sub group	Datsun Type 15						
Marque	Model						
Datsun	Type 15-T						
Body type(s)	Truck Type A		Truck Type B		Chassis		
Power units	722(16)				Timeline		
Final assembly:		Key market	Length (cm)	Drive	Intro.	Start	End	LOST
Japan	Yokohama	Japan	319 (truck)	FR	1936	1936	1938	1938

Type 16

Type 16 Models were similar in most respects to the Type 15. On non-commercial models the chrome strips in the centre of the bonnet vents have been deleted and replaced by chrome strips positioned above and below the vents. Roadster and Phaeton models go back to forward hinged doors (also fitted to some late Type 15 models), as does the coupe which gets new bodywork of 5 window design with a rounded roof and fuller helmet type wings.

Commercial variants continued in Type 15 format.

Model group	Nissan: Datson/Datsun Type 10 to Type 17 revised 1937 Type 16						
Model sub group	Datsun Type 16						
Marque	Model						
Datsun	Type 16						
Body type(s)	Sedan 2dr		Coupe		Phaeton 2dr		
Power units	722(16)				Timeline		
Final assembly:		Key market	Length (cm)	Drive	Intro.	Start	End	LOST
Japan	Yokohama	Japan	319	FR	1937	1937	1938	1938

Model group	Nissan: Datson/Datsun Type 10 to Type 17 revised 1937 Type 16						
Model sub group	Datsun Type 16						
Marque	Model						
Datsun	Type 16 Road-Star						
Body type(s)	Roadster						
Power units	722(16)				Timeline		
Final assembly:		Key market	Length (cm)	Drive	Intro.	Start	End	LOST
Japan	Yokohama	Japan	319	FR	1937	1937	1938	1938

Nissan:Datsun

Datsun
Type 16

16 Sedan

16 Phaeton

16 Road-Star

Nissan:Datsun

Datsun Type 16 Coupe

Nissan: Datsun (Nissan Motor Co)

Type 17

For the 17 model there were few changes. These models can usually be recognised by the standardisation of a wide centre strip in the centre of the grille but this may also feature on Type 15 or 16 models. The strip is usually body colour but chrome was also available. Commercial variants were revised but looked similar to the Type 15 models. The 17-T truck model can be distinguished from the Type 15-T by its plainer cargo box, the 15-T has a raised outline on the box sides following the wheel contours and fastening hoops. The Type 17 Route Van models differ from the Type 15 in having sloping side window tops, squarer cargo area as well as a thicker side running strip.

It should also be noted that restored examples of the Datsun Type 10 to 17 models often have detail inconsistencies with the period equivalent. The factory also incorporated changes to forthcoming models to run-out models of the previous series adding to identity confusion.

Model group	Nissan: Datson/Datsun Type 10 to Type 17 revised 1938 Type 17					
Model sub group	Datsun Type 17 original					
Marque	Model					
Datsun	Type 17					
Body type(s)	Sedan 2dr		Coupe		Phaeton 2dr	
Power units	722(16)					Timeline
Final assembly:	Key market	Length (cm)	Drive	Intro.	Start	End	LOST
Japan Yokohama	Japan	319	FR	1938	1938	1938	1938

Model group	Nissan: Datson/Datsun Type 10 to Type 17 revised 1938 Type 17						
Model sub group	Datsun Type 17 original						
Marque	Model						
Datsun	Type 17 Road-Star						
Body type(s)	Roadster						
Power units	722(16)						Timeline	
Final assembly:	Key market	Length (cm)	Drive	Intro.	Start	End	LOST
Japan Yokohama	Japan	319	FR	1938	1938	1938	1938

Model group	Nissan: Datson/Datsun Type 10 to Type 17 revised 1938 Type 17						
Model sub group	Datsun Type 17 original						
Marque	Model						
Datsun	Type 17-TB Route Van						
Body type(s)	Panel		Window				
Power units	722(16)						Timeline	
Final assembly:	Key market	Length (cm)	Drive	Intro.	Start	End	LOST
Japan Yokohama	Japan	319	FR	1938	1938	1938	1938

Nissan:Datsun

17 Sedan

17 Coupe

Datsun
Type 17

17 Phaeton

Nissan:Datsun

Datsun Type 17

17 Road-Star

17TB Route Van

17-T Chassis with open top box van bodywork

17T-Truck

Nissan: Datsun (Nissan Motor Co)

Model group	Nissan: Datson/Datsun Type 10 to Type 17 revised 1938 Type 17						
Model sub group	Datsun Type 17 original						
Marque	Model						
Datsun	Type 17-T						
Body type(s)	Truck		Chassis				
Power units	722(16)				Timeline		
Final assembly:		Key market	Length (cm)	Drive	Intro.	Start	End	LOST
Japan	Yokohama	Japan	319 (truck)	FR	1938	1938	1944	1944

Type 10 military

Little information is available on these models. The vehicles illustrated are believed to be Scout car and Phaeton military prototypes built on the commercial chassis around 1935 possibly of the Type 13 version.

Model group	Nissan: Datson/Datsun Type 10 to Type 17 Military						
Model sub group	Datsun Type 10 Military						
Marque	Model						
Datsun	Military prototype						
Body type(s)	Roadster		Phaeton 2dr				
Power units	722(16)				Timeline		
Final assembly:		Key market	Length (cm)	Drive	Intro.	Start	End	LOST
Japan	Yokohama				1935	P	1940	P

Datsun NL

The NL models were Nissan's first racing models. The first attempt was the NL-75 based on the Type 14 chassis although the power unit used was the old 747cc unit from the Type 13 with the addition of a twin cam cylinder head and a Roots type supercharger. Suspension was semi-elliptic leaf springs front and rear. The NL-76 was a simpler design largely based on the Type 14 including the use of a reworked version of the Type 14 engine. This model was smaller with a more upright front style than the NL-75. Nissan built two of each model.

Model group	Datsun NL-75						
Marque	Model						
Datsun	NL-75						
Body type(s)	Racing						
Power units	747S(42)				Timeline		
Final assembly:		Key market	Length (cm)	Drive	Intro.	Start	End	LOST
Japan	Yokohama			FR	1936	1936	1936	R

Nissan:Datsun

Datsun
Type 10 series
military prototypes

Scout Car

Military Phaeton

Datsun
NL-75

Nissan: Datsun (Nissan Motor Co)

Model group		Datsun NL-76					
Marque		Model					
Datsun		NL-76					
Body type(s)	Racing						
Power units	722(22)				Timeline		
Final assembly:		Key market	Length (cm)	Drive	Intro.	Start	End	LOST
Japan	Yokohama			FR	1936	1936	1936	R

Nissan (Nissan Motor Co)

Type 50

Medium sized saloon produced in limited numbers.

Model group		Nissan Type 50					
Marque		Model					
Nissan		Type 50					
Body type(s)	Sedan 4dr						
Power units	1468(35)				Timeline		
Final assembly:		Key market	Length (cm)	Drive	Intro.	Start	End	LOST
Japan	Yokohama	Japan		FR	1939	1939	1941	1941

Nissan Type 70

The Nissan Type 70 was essentially a Graham Paige Crusader. On a visit to the United States William Gorham visited a recently closed Graham Paige factory that contained a lot of machinery no longer being used. On Gorham's suggestion, Nissan bought the redundant production line and rights to build the Crusader model for 390,000 US Dollars and installed the tangible assets in their Yokahama factory. This gave Nissan a large car to compete against the American competition. The Model 70 was built in Standard or Special (booted) models, a 7 seat Taxi model using the booted shell, as well as Phaeton and Type 97 military versions. The engine was a Nissan built version of the Graham Paige unit. Approximately 5,500 were built until end of production in 1943 with most being used for military purposes.

Model group		Nissan Model 70					
Marque		Model					
Nissan		Type 70 Sedan					
Body type(s)	Sedan 4dr						
Power units	3670(85)				Timeline		
Final assembly:		Key market	Length (cm)	Drive	Intro.	Start	End	LOST
Japan	Yokohama	Japan	479	FR	1937	1937	1943	1943
Variations:	Sedan: Standard, Special, Taxi						

Nissan:Datsun

Datsun
NL-76

Nissan
Type 50

Nissan

Nissan Type 70

Standard model (right) has sloping rear and exposed wheel. Special version (below) has extended boot with enclosed wheel.

Type 70 used the tooling from the Graham Crusader.

Taxi version with additional seats was similar in style to Special version.

Nissan

Nissan Type 70

Brochure illustrations exaggerated sleekness of the standard car.

Nissan

Nissan Type 70

Type 70 (Model 97 military version)

Type 70 Phaeton

Nissan (Nissan Motor Co)

Model group	Nissan Model 70						
Marque	Model						
Nissan	Type 70 (Model 97)						
Body type(s)	Sedan 4dr						
Power units	3670(85)				Timeline		
Final assembly:		Key market	Length (cm)	Drive	Intro.	Start	End	LOST
Japan Yokohama		Japan	431-472	FR	1937	1937	1943	1943

Model group	Nissan Model 70						
Marque	Model						
Nissan	Type 70 Phaeton						
Body type(s)	Phaeton 4dr						
Power units	3670(85)				Timeline		
Final assembly:		Key market	Length (cm)	Drive	Intro.	Start	End	LOST
Japan Yokohama		Japan	479	FR	1938	1938	1943	1943

Nissan 80-90 series

The first series of Model 80 was the Type 12, named after its introduction in 1937 under the Showa naming system. These models can be recognised by a grille with overlaid bars of descending width going down. These were chrome finished or painted (as an option or when military supplied). This model also used the 3670cc 6-cylinder engine that also went into Type 70 car models. Truck (80T) and Bus (90B) models were available in short (S) or long (L) varieties.

Model group	Nissan Model 80/90 original 12 series						
Marque	Model						
Nissan	Model 80 12TS (swb)						
Body type(s)	Truck						
Power units	3670(85)				Timeline		
Final assembly:		Key market	Length (cm)	Drive	Intro.	Start	End	LOST
Japan Yokohama		Japan	470	FR	1937	1937	1939	1939

Model group	Nissan Model 80/90 original 12 series						
Marque	Model						
Nissan	Model 80 12TL (lwb)						
Body type(s)	Truck						
Power units	3670(85)				Timeline		
Final assembly:		Key market	Length (cm)	Drive	Intro.	Start	End	LOST
Japan Yokohama		Japan	551	FR	1937	1937	1939	1939

Nissan

Nissan
Model 80/90
12 series

Model 80 12TS Truck (swb)

Model 80/90 12 series brochure showing 12TS and 90BL (bus lwb) models.

Nissan

Model 80 12TL Truck (lwb)

Model 80 12BS Bus (swb)

Nissan (Nissan Motor Co)

Model group	Nissan Model 80/90 original 12 series						
Marque	Model						
Nissan	Model 90 12BS Bus swb						
Body type(s)	Bus						
Power units	3670(85)				Timeline		
Final assembly:		Key market	Length (cm)	Drive	Intro.	Start	End	LOST
Japan Yokohama		Japan	470	FR	1937	1937	1939	1939

Model group	Nissan Model 80/90 original 12 series						
Marque	Model						
Nissan	Model 90 12BL Bus lwb						
Body type(s)	Bus						
Power units	3670(85)				Timeline		
Final assembly:		Key market	Length (cm)	Drive	Intro.	Start	End	LOST
Japan Yokohama		Japan	551	FR	1937	1937	1939	1939

Model 81-91-98 series

A modified version of the 80-90 series (Model 81/91) was launched in 1939. This was the 2599 series named after the Imperial year naming system. This version reflected increasing material supply problems and can be recognised by a simpler grille arrangement of multiple horizontal slots. Naming conventions were the same as for the 80/90 series and the model was replaced by the 180 series in 1941.

A further variation of this model was the Type 98 for specialist bodywork applications. This was available in versions A (chassis cab swb), B (chassis cowl swb) and C (chassis cab lwb).

Model group	Nissan Model 80/90 revised 1939 2599 series						
Marque	Model						
Nissan	Model 81 2599 series 99TS Truck swb						
Body type(s)	Truck						
Power units	3670(85)				Timeline		
Final assembly:		Key market	Length (cm)	Drive	Intro.	Start	End	LOST
Japan Yokohama		Japan	470	FR	1939	1939	1941	1941

Model group	Nissan Model 80/90 revised 1939 2599 series						
Marque	Model						
Nissan	Model 81 2599 series 99TL Truck lwb						
Body type(s)	Truck						
Power units	3670(85)				Timeline		
Final assembly:		Key market	Length (cm)	Drive	Intro.	Start	End	LOST
Japan Yokohama		Japan	551	FR	1939	1939	1941	1941

Nissan

Nissan
Model 81/91
2599 series

All images on this page:
Model 81
99TL
Truck
(lwb)

Nissan (Nissan Motor Co)

Model group	Nissan Model 80/90 revised 1939 2599 series							
Marque	Model							
Nissan	Model 91 2599 series 99BS Bus swb							
Body type(s)	Bus							
Power units	3670(85)				Timeline			
Final assembly:		Key market	Length (cm)	Drive	Intro.	Start	End	LOST
Japan	Yokohama	Japan	470	FR	1939	1939	1941	1941

Model group	Nissan Model 80/90 revised 1939 2599 series							
Marque	Model							
Nissan	Model 91 2599 series 99BL Bus lwb							
Body type(s)	Bus							
Power units	3670(85)				Timeline			
Final assembly:		Key market	Length (cm)	Drive	Intro.	Start	End	LOST
Japan	Yokohama	Japan	551	FR	1939	1939	1941	1941

Model group	Nissan Model 80/90 revised 1939 2599 series							
Marque	Model							
Nissan	Model 98 TA Chassis Cab swb							
Body type(s)	Chassis Cab swb							
Power units	3670(85)				Timeline			
Final assembly:		Key market	Length (cm)	Drive	Intro.	Start	End	LOST
Japan	Yokohama	Japan		FR	1939	1939	1941	1941

Model group	Nissan Model 80/90 revised 1939 2599 series							
Marque	Model							
Nissan	Model 98 TB Chassis Cowl swb							
Body type(s)	Chassis Cowl swb							
Power units	3670(85)				Timeline			
Final assembly:		Key market	Length (cm)	Drive	Intro.	Start	End	LOST
Japan	Yokohama	Japan		FR	1939	1939	1941	1941

Model group	Nissan Model 80/90 revised 1939 2599 series							
Marque	Model							
Nissan	Model 98 TC Chassis Cab lwb							
Body type(s)	Chassis Cab lwb							
Power units	3670(85)				Timeline			
Final assembly:		Key market	Length (cm)	Drive	Intro.	Start	End	LOST
Japan	Yokohama	Japan		FR	1939	1939	1941	1941

Nissan

Model 98 Chassis A Tractor Unit

Model 98 Chassis A

Model 98 Chassis B with van body

Model 98 Chassis B

Nissan Model 98 Chassis (2599 series)

Nissan

Model 91BS Bus (swb)

Open and closed bodywork examples shown.

Nissan Model 91/98 (2599 series)

Model 98 Chassis C with van body

Model 91BL Bus (lwb)

Nissin/Nisso

Nissin (later Nisso) was another contemporary sanrinsha vehicle available in a wide range of engine options. Estimated dates.

Model group		Nissin; Nisso						
Model sub group		Nissin						
Marque		Model						
Nissin		500/600/650/750						
Body type(s)	3 wheel cycle truck							
Power units	500	596	650	750	Timeline			
Final assembly:		Key market	Length (cm)	Drive	Intro.	Start	End	LOST
Japan		Japan	280	BMR	1935	1935	1937	1937
Variations: 500, 600, 650, 750								

Model group		Nissin; Nisso						
Model sub group		Nissin						
Marque		Model						
Nissin		675						
Body type(s)	3 wheel cycle truck							
Power units	675				Timeline			
Final assembly:		Key market	Length (cm)	Drive	Intro.	Start	End	LOST
Japan		Japan	280	BMR	1937	1937	1937	1937

Model group		Nissin; Nisso						
Model sub group		Nissin/Nisso revised 1937						
Marque		Model						
Nisso		675/750						
Body type(s)	3 wheel cycle truck							
Power units	675	750			Timeline			
Final assembly:		Key market	Length (cm)	Drive	Intro.	Start	End	LOST
Japan		Japan	280	BMR	1937	1937	1940	1940

Noritu

Sanrinsha vehicle, estimated date and only a 500cc version confirmed.

Model group		Noritu						
Marque		Model						
Noritu		500cc						
Body type(s)	3 wheel cycle truck							
Power units	496				Timeline			
Final assembly:		Key market	Length (cm)	Drive	Intro.	Start	End	LOST
Japan		Japan		BMR	Circa 1935			

Nissin
ニツシン

600cc 1935

600cc

600cc 1936

Nisso

750cc

Noritu

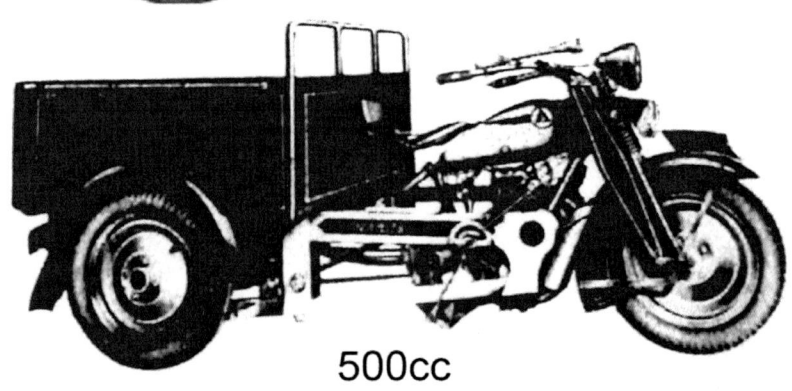
500cc

Ohta (Kohsoku Kikan Kogyo)

Ohta OC/OD models replaced the earlier A series. Earlier OC model used an engine similar to the A series and was available in a restricted range of models. A factory expansion was accompanied by an updated version of the OC – the visually similar OD series with stronger X braced frame and smaller but more powerful engine.

Much like its Datsun competitor, the OD came in a wide variety of models with an almost as wide variety of door opening arrangements which can assist identification: the Standard Sedan (later revised to look less plain) came with external door handles. The De Luxe Sedan (which was more of a slim pillared coupe) featured door handles set in scoops, a style also used on the rounded rear Convertible Model. There was also a Phaeton version with an upright rear end and no external handles (unlike the OC version). Sportiest version was the Roadster model featuring lower sleeker lines, an external spare wheel and the concealed door handle arrangement.

Truck and Van models continued with the Van model also being available with rear side windows or with an open top.

Ohta also built a small racing model for the All-Japan Automobile Competition in 1936 at Tamagawa Speedway.

> Ohta model available in this period covered in previous volumes:
>
> - Ohta A, 1933-1935, Volume 1

Model group			Ohta OC					
Marque			Model					
Ohta			OC					
Body type(s)	Phaeton 2dr		Van					
Power units	748(12.5)					Timeline		
Final assembly:		Key market	Length (cm)	Drive	Intro.	Start	End	LOST
Japan	Omori, Tokyo	Japan	319	FR	1936	1936	1937	1937

Model group			Ohta OC					
Marque			Model					
Ohta			OC Pick up					
Body type(s)	Pick up							
Power units	748(12.5)					Timeline		
Final assembly:		Key market	Length (cm)	Drive	Intro.	Start	End	LOST
Japan	Omori, Tokyo	Japan	319	FR	1935	1935	1937	1937

Ohta

OC Phaeton

OD Standard Sedan
1937

OD Standard Sedan
1937-1940

Ohta (Kohsoku Kikan Kogyo)

Model group	\multicolumn{5}{c}{Ohta OD}				
Marque	\multicolumn{5}{c}{Model}				
Ohta	\multicolumn{5}{c}{OD}				
Body type(s)	Standard Sedan 2dr							
Power units	736(15-16P)				Timeline			
Final assembly:		Key market	Length (cm)	Drive	Intro.	Start	End	LOST
Japan	Omori, Tokyo	Japan	319	FR	1937	1937	1937	1937

Model group	\multicolumn{5}{c}{Ohta OD}				
Marque	\multicolumn{5}{c}{Model}				
Ohta	\multicolumn{5}{c}{OD}				
Body type(s)	Standard Sedan 2dr	De Luxe Sedan 2dr		Convertible 2str				
	Roadster	Phaeton 4str						
Power units	736(15-16P)				Timeline			
Final assembly:		Key market	Length (cm)	Drive	Intro.	Start	End	LOST
Japan	Omori, Tokyo	Japan	319	FR	1937	1937	1940	1940

Model group	\multicolumn{5}{c}{Ohta OD}				
Marque	\multicolumn{5}{c}{Model}				
Ohta	\multicolumn{5}{c}{OD}				
Body type(s)	Standard Route Van (panel)	Route Van (window)		Truck				
Power units	736(15-16P)				Timeline			
Final assembly:		Key market	Length (cm)	Drive	Intro.	Start	End	LOST
Japan	Omori, Tokyo	Japan	319	FR	1937	1937	1942	1942

Model group	\multicolumn{5}{c}{Ohta racing}				
Marque	\multicolumn{5}{c}{Model}				
Ohta	\multicolumn{5}{c}{750cc}				
Body type(s)	Racing							
Power units	748(23)				Timeline			
Final assembly:		Key market	Length (cm)	Drive	Intro.	Start	End	LOST
Japan	Omori, Tokyo	Japan		FR	1936	1936	1936	R

Ohta

Ohta OD

OD Convertible

OD Phaeton

OD De Luxe Sedan

Ohta

Ohta
OD

OD Roadster

OD Standard Route Van (open top)

OD Route Van

Ohta

OD Standard Route Van

OD Standard Truck

OD Standard Truck

750cc racing model

Okamoto

Okamoto were involved with the Kurogane 95 project but also made three military scout car prototypes with their own brand name. These used a V-twin air cooled power unit that may have been related to the Kurogane unit.

Model group			Okamoto				
Marque			Model				
Okamoto			1200				
Body type(s)	Roadster						
Power units	1200				Timeline		
Final assembly:		Key market	Length (cm)	Drive	Intro.	Start	End	LOST
Japan		Japan				Circa 1937		

OS

Another of the small electric vehicle producers. Limited information

Model group			OS				
Marque			Model				
OS							
Body type(s)	Sedan 2dr						
Power units	E				Timeline		
Final assembly:		Key market	Length (cm)	Drive	Intro.	Start	End	LOST
Japan	Osaka	Japan			1939	1939	1940	1940

Raito (Raito Automobile Co)

Producer of small car and commercial vehicles similar to those of Datsun and Ohta. Some degree of popularity throughout the thirties but died out during this period.

> Raito model available in this period covered in previous volumes:
>
> - Raito Pick Up, 1932-1937, Volume 1

Model group			Raito				
Marque			Model				
Raito			Spirit				
Body type(s)	Sedan 2dr		Van		Truck		
Power units	732(17)				Timeline		
Final assembly:		Key market	Length (cm)	Drive	Intro.	Start	End	LOST
Japan	Tokyo	Japan	280	FR	1937	1937	1938	1938

Okamoto

1200

OS

Raito

Spirit Sedan

Van

Truck

Rikuo (Rikuo Nainenki)

Rikuo evolved from the Japanese Harley-Davidson. The brand continued to 1962 but sanrinsha type vehicles were dropped in 1949 following some post-war production. Rikuo were another company that put forward a small military scout car prototype - the Type 98.

Model group		Rikuo						
Marque		Model						
Rikuo		750RD Servicar						
Body type(s)	3 wheel cycle truck							
Power units	747				Timeline			
Final assembly:		Key market	Length (cm)	Drive	Intro.	Start	End	LOST
Japan	Tokyo	Japan	280	BMR	1937	1937	1942	1942

Model group		Rikuo						
Marque		Model						
Rikuo		1200cc						
Body type(s)	3 wheel cycle truck							
Power units	1213				Timeline			
Final assembly:		Key market	Length (cm)	Drive	Intro.	Start	End	LOST
Japan	Tokyo	Japan	280	BMR	1937	1937	1942	1942

Model group		Rikuo						
Marque		Model						
Rikuo		Type 98						
Body type(s)	Roadster							
Power units	1300				Timeline			
Final assembly:		Key market	Length (cm)	Drive	Intro.	Start	End	LOST
Japan	Tokyo	Japan		F4	1938	P	1940	P

Rokko (Kawasaki Rolling Stock)

Rokko products listed were evolutions of earlier models. Diesel engines were apparently available from 1941 but specification for these unknown and the company ceased production the following year.

> Rokko models available in this period covered in previous volumes:
> - KP, 1931-1937, Volume 1
> - KT, 1932-1937, Volume 1
> - KB, 1932-1937, Volume 1
> - ST, 1932-1937, Volume 1

Rikuo

750RD Servicar

1200cc

Type 98

Rokko

KT-20 Chassis

Rokko (Kawasaki Rolling Stock)

Model group		Rokko KP revised 1937						
Marque		Model						
Rokko		KP-52A Sedan						
Body type(s)	Sedan 4dr							
Power units	4891(66)	5071(90-100)			Timeline			
Final assembly:		Key market	Length (cm)	Drive	Intro.	Start	End	LOST
Japan	Kawasaki	Japan		FR	1937	1937	1942	1942

Model group		Rokko KP revised 1937						
Marque		Model						
Rokko		KP-52 Phaeton						
Body type(s)	Phaeton 4dr							
Power units	4891(66)	5071(90-100)			Timeline			
Final assembly:		Key market	Length (cm)	Drive	Intro.	Start	End	LOST
Japan	Kawasaki	Japan		FR	1937	1937	1942	1942

Model group		Rokko KT; Rokko ST; Rokko KB revised 1937						
Marque		Model						
Rokko		KT						
Body type(s)	Truck chassis							
Power units	4390(60)				Timeline			
Final assembly:		Key market	Length (cm)	Drive	Intro.	Start	End	LOST
Japan	Kawasaki	Japan		FR	1937	1937	1942	1942
Variations: KT-15 (1.5t), KT-20 (2.0t)								

Model group		Rokko KT; Rokko ST; Rokko KB revised 1937						
Marque		Model						
Rokko		ST-20						
Body type(s)	Truck chassis							
Power units	4390(60)				Timeline			
Final assembly:		Key market	Length (cm)	Drive	Intro.	Start	End	LOST
Japan	Kawasaki	Japan		FR	1937	1937	1942	1942

Model group		Rokko KT; Rokko ST; Rokko KB revised 1937						
Marque		Model						
Rokko		KB-20						
Body type(s)	Bus chassis							
Power units	4891(66)				Timeline			
Final assembly:		Key market	Length (cm)	Drive	Intro.	Start	End	LOST
Japan	Kawasaki	Japan		FR	1937	1937	1942	1942

Rokko

KP-24 Phaeton

Four cylinder model with Packard like styling from the 1931-37 model series.

KP-52A Sedan

KP-52 models shown are from the revised 1937 on model series.

KP-52 Phaeton

Showa-Go

Model group	Showa-GO						
Marque	Model						
Showa-GO	750cc						
Body type(s)	3 wheel cycle truck						
Power units	750				Timeline		
Final assembly:		Key market	Length (cm)	Drive	Intro.	Start	End	LOST
Japan Nagoya		Japan		BMR	Circa 1935			

Success (Osawa Shokai)

Estimated dates. Engines came from a variety of suppliers: 500 from OKB, 600 from BSA and 650 from JAC. This entry also updates the entry in volume 1 of this book series.

Model group	Success revised 1935							
Marque	Model							
Success	Rearcar							
Body type(s)	3 wheel cycle truck							
Power units	500	600	650		Timeline			
Final assembly:		Key market	Length (cm)	Drive	Intro.	Start	End	LOST
Japan Tokyo		Japan		BMR	1935	1935	1938	1938

Suzuki

Model group	Suzuki ZZZ 1937						
Marque	Model						
Suzuki	Prototype						
Body type(s)	Phaeton 2dr						
Power units	800(13)				Timeline		
Final assembly:		Key market	Length (cm)	Drive	Intro.	Start	End	LOST
Japan Hamamatsu		Japan			1937	P	1938	P

Takara

Model group	Takara						
Marque	Model						
Takara	Truck						
Body type(s)	Truck						
Power units	E				Timeline		
Final assembly:		Key market	Length (cm)	Drive	Intro.	Start	End	LOST
Japan Osaka		Japan	280		1937	1937	1940	1940

Showa-Go

750cc

Success

Rearcar 600 1935

Suzuki

Phaeton prototype

Takara

Electric truck

Toyota: Toyoda Automatic Loom Works (cars)

Note: Toyoda became Toyota Motor Co. in 1937.

AA/AB

Toyoda built three A1 prototypes that copied Chrysler Airflow models for the bodywork, Chevrolet for the engine and Ford for the chassis. As with the Nissan 70 this amalgam of American ideas clearly positioned this model as a competitor for US products. The A1 was refined into the production AA model that was later re-named as a Toyota and further developed into the split screen AC model. Production figures were 1,404 for the sedan and 353 for the AB phaeton model. Toyoda models were made at Nagoya, Toyota models (initially) at Kariya.

Production dates for the AB/ABR differ widely but the most likely termination date is 1938. This would tie in with the later production shift to the Koromo plant completed in 1938. Most early models were supplied in ABR format for military use. The doors on the Phaeton were conventionally arranged which compared with the rear coach door arrangement used on the sedan version. The A1/AA/AB models used the A Type engine but the revised B Type version of the engine was used in Koromo built models with a power increase from 1940.

AA models featured a sloping rear end; however the surviving model currently in the Louwman Museum in the Netherlands features a protruding boot. Some manufacturers (e.g. Nissan, Ford) offered booted and non-booted rear styles but research for this publication has failed to uncover any availability of this feature on the Toyota. Given the non standard nature of many parts on the Louwman example this anomaly is likely to be a post production modification.

Model group	Toyoda A1; Toyoda/Toyota AA; AB; Toyota AC original							
Model sub group	Toyoda A1							
Marque	Model							
Toyoda	A1							
Body type(s)	Sedan 4dr							
Power units	3389(62)					Timeline		
Final assembly:		Key market	Length (cm)	Drive	Intro.	Start	End	LOST
Japan	Nagoya		479	FR	1935	P	P	P

Model group	Toyoda A1; Toyoda/Toyota AA; AB; Toyota AC original							
Model sub group	Toyoda AA original							
Marque	Model							
Toyoda	AA							
Body type(s)	Sedan 4dr							
Power units	3389(65)					Timeline		
Final assembly:		Key market	Length (cm)	Drive	Intro.	Start	End	LOST
Japan	Nagoya	Japan	479	FR	1936	1936	1936	1936

Toyoda/Toyota

Toyoda A1

Toyoda AA

Toyoda AA brochure

Louwman Museum
Toyoda AA with boot

Toyoda/Toyota

Toyota AA

Koromo plant

Toyota: Toyoda Automatic Loom Works (cars)

Model group	Toyoda A1; Toyoda/Toyota AA; AB; Toyota AC original							
Model sub group	Toyoda AB original							
Marque	Model							
Toyoda	AB							
Body type(s)	Phaeton 4dr							
Power units	3389(65)				Timeline			
Final assembly:		Key market	Length (cm)	Drive	Intro.	Start	End	LOST
Japan	Nagoya	Japan	479	FR	1936	1936	1936	1936

Model group	Toyoda A1; Toyoda/Toyota AA; AB; Toyota AC original							
Model sub group	Toyoda ABR original							
Marque	Model							
Toyoda	ABR							
Body type(s)	Phaeton 4dr							
Power units	3389(65)				Timeline			
Final assembly:		Key market	Length (cm)	Drive	Intro.	Start	End	LOST
Japan	Nagoya	Japan	479	FR	1936	1936	1936	1936

Model group	Toyoda A1; Toyoda/Toyota AA; AB; Toyota AC revised 1936							
Model sub group	Toyota AA revised 1936							
Marque	Model							
Toyota	AA							
Body type(s)	Sedan 4dr							
Power units	3389(65)				Timeline			
Final assembly:		Key market	Length (cm)	Drive	Intro.	Start	End	LOST
Japan	Kariya	Japan	479	FR	1936	1936	1938	1938

Model group	Toyoda A1; Toyoda/Toyota AA; AB; Toyota AC revised 1936							
Model sub group	Toyota AB revised 1936							
Marque	Model							
Toyota	AB							
Body type(s)	Phaeton 4dr							
Power units	3389(65)				Timeline			
Final assembly:		Key market	Length (cm)	Drive	Intro.	Start	End	LOST
Japan	Kariya	Japan	479	FR	1936	1936	1938	1938

Model group	Toyoda A1; Toyoda/Toyota AA; AB; Toyota AC revised 1936							
Model sub group	Toyota ABR revised 1936							
Marque	Model							
Toyota	ABR							
Body type(s)	Phaeton 4dr							
Power units	3389(65)				Timeline			
Final assembly:		Key market	Length (cm)	Drive	Intro.	Start	End	LOST
Japan	Kariya	Japan	479	FR	1936	1936	1938	1938

Toyoda/Toyota

Toyoda AB

The beige model uses the three slot bonnet vents design used on later (37-38?) models that matches the similar arrangement on the saloon models. This vehicle uses the same wheels as the Toyoda version shown. This style seems to have been used on most phaetons.

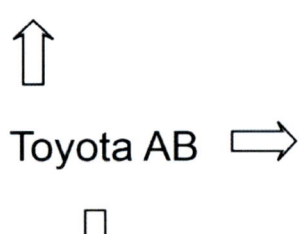

Toyota AB

Toyota (Toyota Motor Co) (cars)

Koromo plant model, the 78bhp unit was used from 1940.

Model group	Toyoda A1; Toyoda/Toyota AA; AB; Toyota AC revised 1938						
Model sub group	Toyota AA revised 1938						
Marque	Model						
Toyota	AA						
Body type(s)	Sedan 4dr						
Power units	3389(75)	3389(78)			Timeline		
Final assembly:		Key market	Length (cm)	Drive	Intro.	Start	End	LOST
Japan	Koromo	Japan	479	FR	1938	1938	1943	1943

Toyota AE

The AE was a mid-sized car developed at the request of the Ministry of Commerce and Industry. Production was limited to 76 units over two years mainly because of government restrictions on passenger car production. This model used a 2.3 litre power unit called the C Type.

Model group	Toyota AE						
Marque	Model						
Toyota	AE						
Body type(s)	Sedan 4dr						
Power units	2258(50)				Timeline		
Final assembly:		Key market	Length (cm)	Drive	Intro.	Start	End	LOST
Japan	Koromo	Japan	450	FR	1939	1941	1943	1943

Toyota: Toyoda Automatic Loom Works (commercials)

Toyoda G1

The Toyoda G1 was another vehicle powered by the A Type engine and like the A1 sedan had style features copied from the American vehicles it was in competition with. As well as the Chevrolet based engine, Chevrolet also provided inspiration for the front suspension. The chassis and rear suspension were based on the Ford AA model. The factory cab was based on a Diamond T design. Carrying capacity was 1.5t. Production shifted from the Toyoda Automatic Loom Works plant at Nagoya to the new Kariya plant during 1936.

Toyoda/Toyota

Toyota
AE

Toyoda/Toyota

G1 brochure

Toyoda
G1

Extended cab on G1
Chassis base

G1 metal cab

Toyota: Toyoda Automatic Loom Works (commercials)

Model group		Toyoda G1, Toyoda DA						
Marque		Model						
Toyoda		G1						
Body type(s)	Truck	Chassis						
Power units	3389(65)				Timeline			
Final assembly:		Key market	Length (cm)	Drive	Intro.	Start	End	LOST
Japan	Nagoya/Kariya	Japan	595	FR	1935	1935	1936	1936

Toyota GA/GY

The GA is an updated version of the G1 with 2t capacity and can be recognised by the less extreme dip at the top of the radiator. The GY is a swb version of the GA. The key differences are:

GY is 3.5t gvw model with single rear wheels and 330cm wheelbase.

GA is 4t gvw model with dual rear wheels and 359cm wheelbase

Some of these may have built at the new Koromo plant but evidence found is conflicting on this point.

Model group		Toyota GA; Toyota GY; Toyota DA						
Model sub group		Toyota GA						
Marque		Model						
Toyota		GA						
Body type(s)	Truck	Chassis						
Power units	3389(65)				Timeline			
Final assembly:		Key market	Length (cm)	Drive	Intro.	Start	End	LOST
Japan	Kariya	Japan	595	FR	1936	1936	1940	1940

Model group		Toyota GA; Toyota GY; Toyota DA						
Model sub group		Toyota GY						
Marque		Model						
Toyota		GY						
Body type(s)	Truck	Chassis						
Power units	3389(65)				Timeline			
Final assembly:		Key market	Length (cm)	Drive	Intro.	Start	End	LOST
Japan	Kariya	Japan	537 (truck)	FR	1937	1937	1940	1940

Toyoda/Toyota

GA metal cab

Toyota GA

GA Chassis

GA single cab on chassis

GA brochure

Toyoda/Toyota

Toyota GY Open Cab

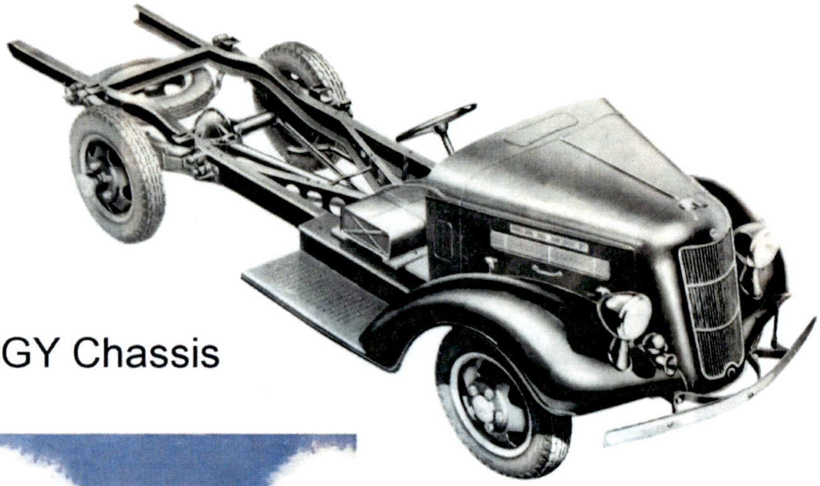

Toyota GY Chassis

Toyota GY brochure image showing the grille style used on GA, GY and later DA models.

Toyota GY

Toyota: Toyoda Automatic Loom Works (commercials)

Toyoda/Toyota DA

Bus equivalent of the G series trucks, the early models were built at Nagoya, later models the Kariya plant. Early models were based on the G1 truck with similar styling and chassis dimensions but featuring a low floor. From late 1936 the DA model was based on the GA/GY models and copied the style and chassis dimensions of these models. These later models were built at Kariya but some may have been made at the Koromo plant. The later versions came as a lwb based on the GA with dual rear wheels or as a swb (GY based) model with single rear wheels from 1937.

Model group		Toyoda G1, Toyoda DA						
Model sub group		Toyoda DA original						
Marque		Model						
Toyoda		DA Bus Chassis						
Body type(s)	Bus chassis							
Power units	3389(62)					Timeline		
Final assembly:		Key market	Length (cm)	Drive	Intro.	Start	End	LOST
Japan	Nagoya/Kariya	Japan	670	FR	1936	1936	1936	1936

Model group		Toyota GA; Toyota GY; Toyota DA						
Model sub group		Toyota DA revised 1936						
Marque		Model						
Toyota		DA Bus Chassis lwb						
Body type(s)	Bus chassis lwb							
Power units	3389(62)					Timeline		
Final assembly:		Key market	Length (cm)	Drive	Intro.	Start	End	LOST
Japan	Kariya	Japan	670 (lwb)	FR	1936	1936	1940	1940

Model group		Toyota GA; Toyota GY; Toyota DA						
Model sub group		Toyota DA revised 1936						
Marque		Model						
Toyota		DA Bus Chassis swb						
Body type(s)	Bus chassis swb							
Power units	3389(62)					Timeline		
Final assembly:		Key market	Length (cm)	Drive	Intro.	Start	End	LOST
Japan	Kariya	Japan		FR	1937	1937	1940	1940

Toyoda/Toyota

Toyota DA Chassis lwb

Toyoda/Toyota DA

Toyoda DA models follow G1 Truck style.

DA publicity image from 1937 showing the later Toyota model in the GA style.

Toyota (Toyota Motor Co) (commercials)

Toyota GB/HB/DB

The GB was an updated version of the GA using the B series (modified A series) engine. The 78 bhp power upgrade applied from 1940. Wheelbase on this model was 361cm. HB model was a short wheelbase version (330cm). Some GB models were made in China from 1939. For 1939 the GB model received revised styling with a pointed front. The bus chassis is based on the HB model. There was also a similar DM bus model, too large for this volume - a higher capacity evolution of the DA bus with the revised B engine and GB/HB front end style.

Model group	Toyota GB; Toyota HB original							
Model sub group	Toyota GB original							
Marque	Model							
Toyota	GB							
Body type(s)	Truck		Chassis					
Power units	3389(75)	3389(78)			Timeline			
Final assembly:	Key market	Length (cm)		Drive	Intro.	Start	End	LOST
Japan Koromo	Japan	641 (truck)		FR	1938	1938	1939	1939

Model group	Toyota GB; Toyota HB; Toyota DB revised 1939							
Model sub group	Toyota GB revised 1939							
Marque	Model							
Toyota	GB							
Body type(s)	Truck		Chassis					
Power units	3389(75)	3389(78)			Timeline			
Final assembly:	Key market	Length (cm)		Drive	Intro.	Start	End	LOST
Japan Koromo	Japan	641 (truck)		FR	1939	1939	1942	1942

Model group	Toyota GB; Toyota HB revised 1939							
Model sub group	Toyota HB							
Marque	Model							
Toyota	HB							
Body type(s)	Truck		Chassis					
Power units	3389(75)	3389(78)			Timeline			
Final assembly:	Key market	Length (cm)		Drive	Intro.	Start	End	LOST
Japan Koromo	Japan	612 (truck)		FR	1939	1939	1941	1941

Model group	Toyota GB; Toyota HB; Toyota DB revised 1939							
Model sub group	Toyota DB							
Marque	Model							
Toyota	DB Bus Chassis							
Body type(s)	Bus chassis							
Power units	3389(75)				Timeline			
Final assembly:	Key market	Length (cm)		Drive	Intro.	Start	End	LOST
Japan Koromo	Japan	650		FR	1939	1939	1941	1941

Toyoda/Toyota

Toyota GB 1938

Toyota GB 1939

Toyoda/Toyota

Toyota DB

Toyota DB Bus models (custom bodywork on chassis)

Toyota DB/HB Chassis

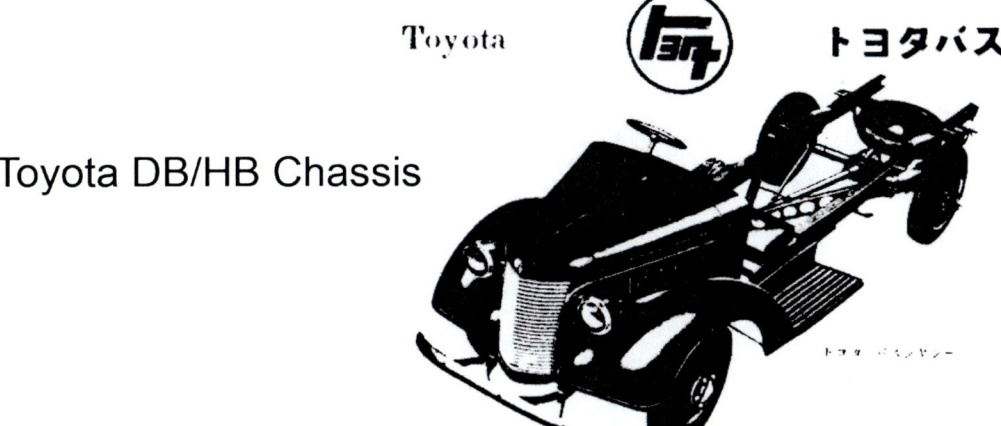

Tsubasa (NABCO)

Tsubasa products in this period were still being produced by Nippon Air Brake Co (NABCO) but later became an independent company. The models covered in this volume were Tsubasa own products unlike most of the models covered in volume 1 of this series which were essentially copies of Daihatsu products. Dates are estimated for these models.

> Tsubasa model available in this period covered in previous volumes:
> - HK1, 1933-1935, Volume 1

Model group		Tsubasa (NABCO) original						
Marque		Model						
Tsubasa		GD-1						
Body type(s)	3 wheel cycle truck							
Power units	650					Timeline		
Final assembly:		Key market	Length (cm)	Drive	Intro.	Start	End	LOST
Japan	Osaka	Japan	205	BMR	1935	1935	1936	1936

Model group		Tsubasa (NABCO) original						
Marque		Model						
Tsubasa		GV-1						
Body type(s)	3 wheel cycle truck							
Power units	749					Timeline		
Final assembly:		Key market	Length (cm)	Drive	Intro.	Start	End	LOST
Japan	Osaka	Japan	205	BMR	1935	1935	1936	1936

Model group		Tsubasa (NABCO) revised 1936						
Marque		Model						
Tsubasa		GD-1						
Body type(s)	3 wheel cycle truck							
Power units	650					Timeline		
Final assembly:		Key market	Length (cm)	Drive	Intro.	Start	End	LOST
Japan	Osaka	Japan		BMR	1936	1936	1942	1942

Model group		Tsubasa (NABCO) revised 1936						
Marque		Model						
Tsubasa		GV-1						
Body type(s)	3 wheel cycle truck							
Power units	749					Timeline		
Final assembly:		Key market	Length (cm)	Drive	Intro.	Start	End	LOST
Japan	Osaka	Japan		BMR	1936	1936	1942	1942

Tsubasa

1935

1936

1940

Tsukuba (Tokyo Jidosha Seizo)

The front wheel drive Tsukuba evolved from the earlier Roland car. Similar to the Ford Eight and available in a number of body styles. Around 130 produced with some exports to China.

Model group			Tsukuba				
Marque			Model				
Tsukuba			Sedan 2dr				
Body type(s)	Sedan 2dr		Roadster		Cabriolet 2dr		
	Phaeton 2dr		Estate 3dr		Truck		
	Chassis						
Power units	736(7-18)				Timeline		
Final assembly:		Key market	Length (cm)	Drive	Intro.	Start	End	LOST
Japan		Tokyo	Japan	280	FF	1935	1935	1938	1938

Welby (KRS)

The Welby was a contemporary sanrinsha type vehicle using JAP engines. Listed in Pomchi volume 1 as KRS Welby, the latter name became more prominent in later years.

Model group			Welby revised 1935				
Marque			Model				
Welby			500/650/670				
Body type(s)	3 wheel cycle truck						
Power units	500	650	670		Timeline		
Final assembly:		Key market	Length (cm)	Drive	Intro.	Start	End	LOST
Japan		Kyoto	Japan		BMR	1935	1935	1940	1940

Yamarta (Osaka Minata Nakijima Seisakusho)

Yamarta disappeared around 1937. Sanrinsha produced from 1929 but started in 1916 in Osaka adding motors to non powered tricycles. Sometimes referred to as Yamata.

> Yamarta model available in this period covered in previous volumes:
> - Rear-Car 500cc, 1931-1935, Volume 1

Model group			Yamarta revised 1935				
Marque			Model				
Yamarta			Rear-car				
Body type(s)	3 wheel cycle truck						
Power units	500	600	649	750	Timeline		
Final assembly:		Key market	Length (cm)	Drive	Intro.	Start	End	LOST
Japan		Nakajima	Japan	280	BMR	1935	1935	1937	1937

Tsukuba

Sedan 1935

Sedan 1938

Welby

1936

Yamarta

1935

1935

1936

Bibliography

The intention of this publication is to provide a basic overview of what was made and when. For more detailed information on the products and companies covered please consult the following recommended additional reading:

English language:

Beaulieu Encyclopaedia of the Automobile, G.N. Georgano, 2000 (for marque histories).

The Complete History of the Japanese Car, Ruiz, Portland House, 1986 (for industry history).

Japanese Language:

The 20th Century Of the Japanese Automobile, Yaesu Shuppan, 2000 (potted coverage of wide selection of models).

Small and light trucks annual (translated title), Yoji Katsuragi, GP Planning Centre, 2006 (for light trucks).

Retrospective of auto tricycle history (translated title), GP Planning Centre, 2000 (for 3-wheelers).

Domestic three wheeled vehicle catalogue 1930-1974 (translated), Kazuo Kaseki, 2010 (for 3-wheelers).

Japanese automobile handbook annuals, various years (annual catalogue of key products for public).

French Language:

Nissan Planete Automobile, Bernard Vermeylen, ETAI, 2014 (for Nissan history).

German Language:

Autos made in Japan, Jan Norbye, 1991 (for industry history).

Nissan seit 1933, Joachim Kuch, Motor buch Verlag, 2005 (for Nissan history).

Websites:

earlydatsun.com (for wide coverage of early Datsun models).

Image sources

The purpose of this publication is to portray the featured vehicles in the form they were supplied by the manufacturer, therefore wherever possible the main source of information has been the product promotional literature published by the companies covered by this publication.

The publisher has tried to identify the copyright holders of images used in this publication. If you are the owner of an image that has not been credited, please contact the publisher for this to be rectified in subsequent editions.

Image sources with page number location: Asahi Nainenki: 51 (all), Asia: 10 (middle/bottom); Atsuta: 12 (except bottom); Crabbe: 12 (bottom); Daihatsu Motor Company: 14 (all except bottom), 16 (top/middle); Denka: 16 (bottom), Editor's collection: 14 (bottom), 25 (top), 56 (all), 59 (centre), 66 (2nd), 67 (2nd), 90 (middle), 80 (bottom), 93 (2nd), 106 (2nd), 110 (top), 114 (2nd), 143 (top), Ford Motor Co.(Japan): 18 (all), 20 (all), 21 (all), 22 (all), 25 (middle/bottom), Fujiya: 27 (all), General Motors Japan: 30 (all), Graham-Paige: 96 (bottom), Hijiri: 34 (except bottom), Hirano: 34 (bottom), Hitachi-Federal: 36 (except bottom); Hitakashi: 36 (bottom), Hoxon: 38 (1st, 2nd), Hyogo: 38 (middle); Ikegai: 38 (4th, 5th), JAC: 53 (top), Jidosha Kogyo: 45 (bottom), 48 (all), 49 (all), Kawasaki Rolling Stock: 119 (bottom),121 (all), Kohsoku Kikan Kogyo: 110 (middle/bottom), 112 (all), 113 (all), 114 (1st, 3rd, 4th), Kokueki: 53 (middle/bottom), KRS: 143 (bottom), Kyosan Electric Manufacturing: 62 (all); 63 (all), 64 (top), Louwman Museum: 125 (bottom), Matsuo: 64 (middle/bottom), Mitsubishi Heavy Industries: 71 (top), Miyata Works: 10 (top), 71 (middle), Mizuno Metal Works: 71 (bottom), MSA: 73 (1st, 2nd), Nagoya Automotive Works: 73 (3rd, 4th), 74 (top), Nakajima Seisakusho: 74 (2nd, 3rd, 4th), NEC Automotive Works: 76 (top), Nikko: 76 (middle/bottom), New Era: 55 (top); Nihon Nainenki: 55 (middle/bottom), 58 (all), 59 (top/bottom), Nippon Air Brake: 141 (all); Nissan Heritage Collection: 79 (top), 83 (bottom), 84 (top), 87 (1st, 2nd), 88 (top), 90 (top/bottom), 91 (1st, 3rd), 96 (1st), 98 (bottom), 105 (3rd), Nissan Motor Company: 78 (all), 79 (middle/bottom), 80 (all), 82 (all), 83 (top/middle), 84 (middle/bottom), 85 (all), 87 (3rd, 4th), 88 (middle/bottom), 91 (2nd, 4th), 93 (except 2nd), 95 (all), 96 (2nd, 3rd), 97 (all), 98 (top/middle), 100 (all), 101 (all), 103 (all), 105 (all except 3rd), 106 (all), Nissin/Nisso: 108 (all except bottom), Noritu: 108 (bottom), Okamoto: 116 (top), OS: 116 (bottom), Raito: 117 (all), Osaka Minata Nakijima Seisakusho: 144 (all), Rikuo Nainenki: 119 (all except bottom), Seiki Kogyo: 32 (all), Showa-Go: 123 (top), Success: 123 (2nd), Suzuki: 123 (3rd), Takara: 123 (bottom), Tokyo Automobile Industries: 41 (all), 42 (all), 43 (all), Tokyo Gas and Electric: 45 (top/middle), Tokyo Jidosha Seizo: 143 (middle), Toyo Kogyo: 66 (all except 2nd); 67 (all except 2nd); 69 (all),Toyota Automobile Museum: 126 (bottom), 128 (3rd, 4th), 130 (3rd), Toyota Motor Co: 125 (all except bottom), 126 (all except bottom), 128 (1st, 2nd), 130 (all except 3rd), 131 (all), 133 (all), 134 (all), 136 (all), 138 (all), 139 (all),

All rights reserved. No part of this publication may be reproduced or transmitted in any form or by any means without permission in writing from the publisher.

© Pomchi Press Ltd 2017

Published by: Pomchi Press Ltd, Yate, United Kingdom.

Made in United States
North Haven, CT
29 August 2022